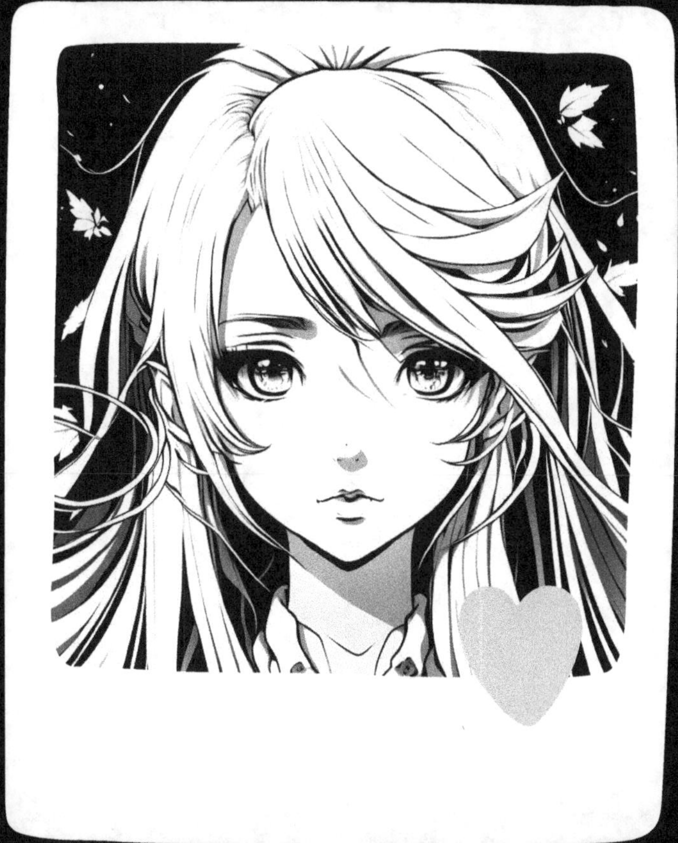

TOKYO STREETS

CAPI CAMP ESTUDIOS

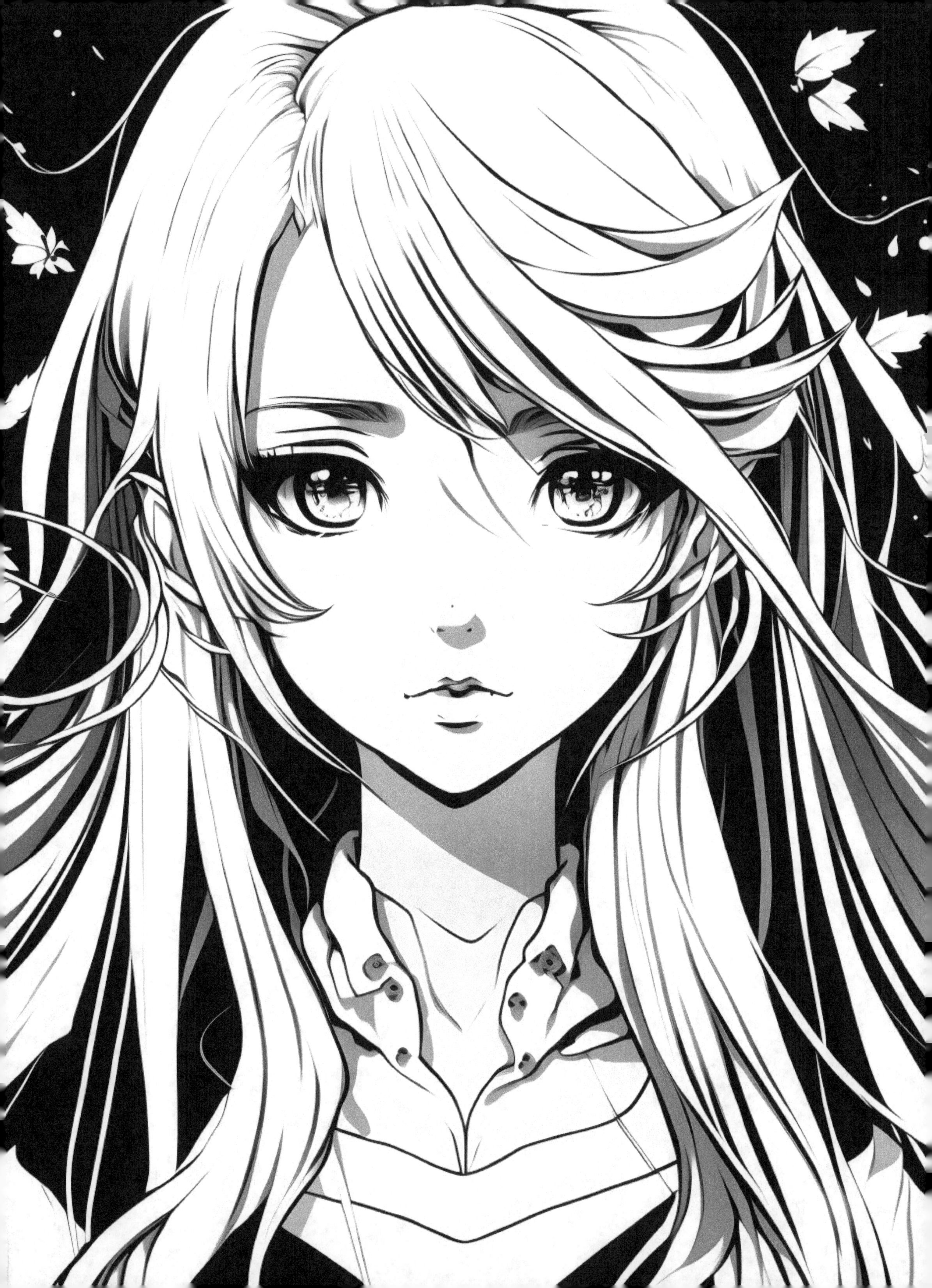

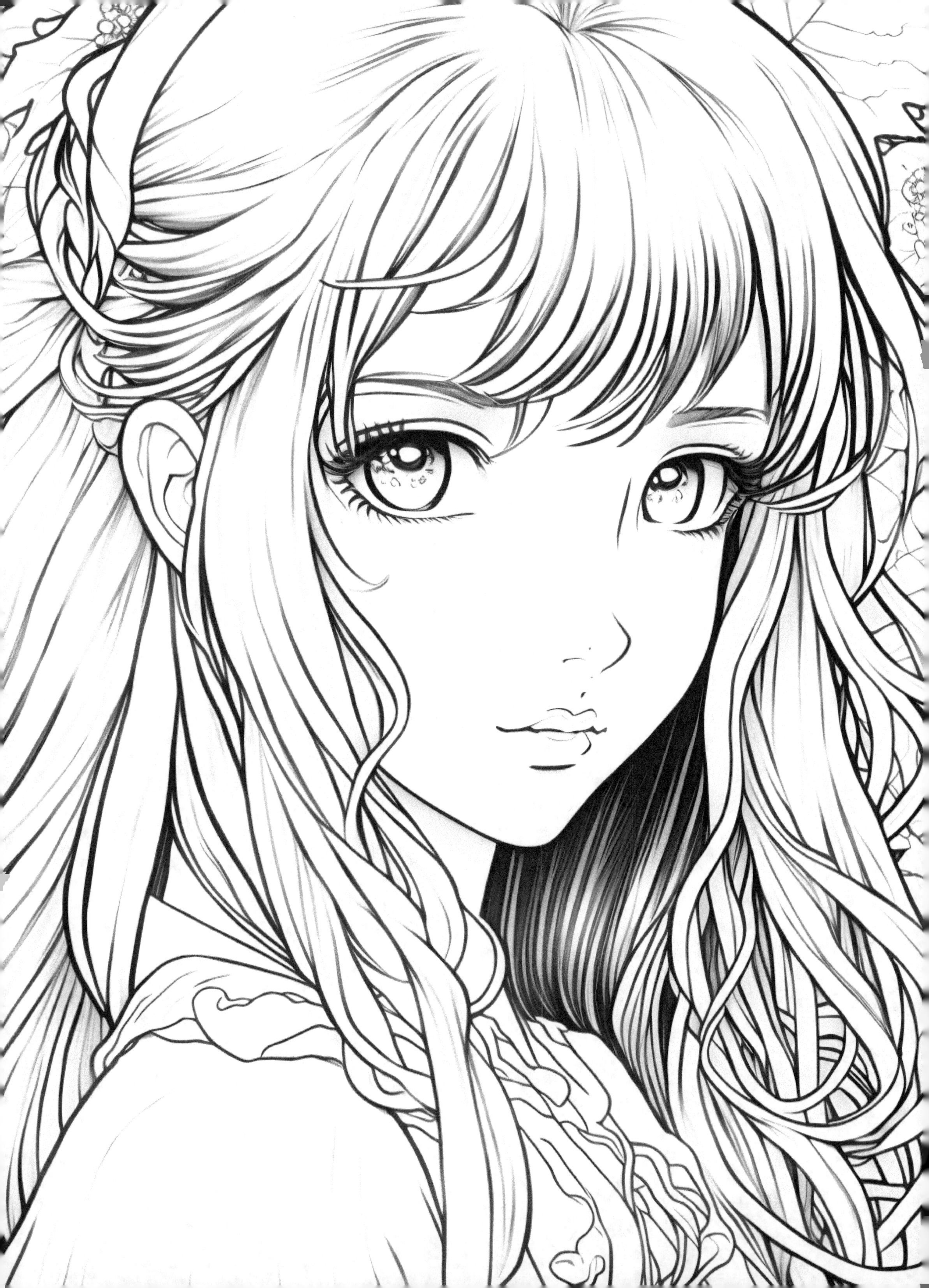

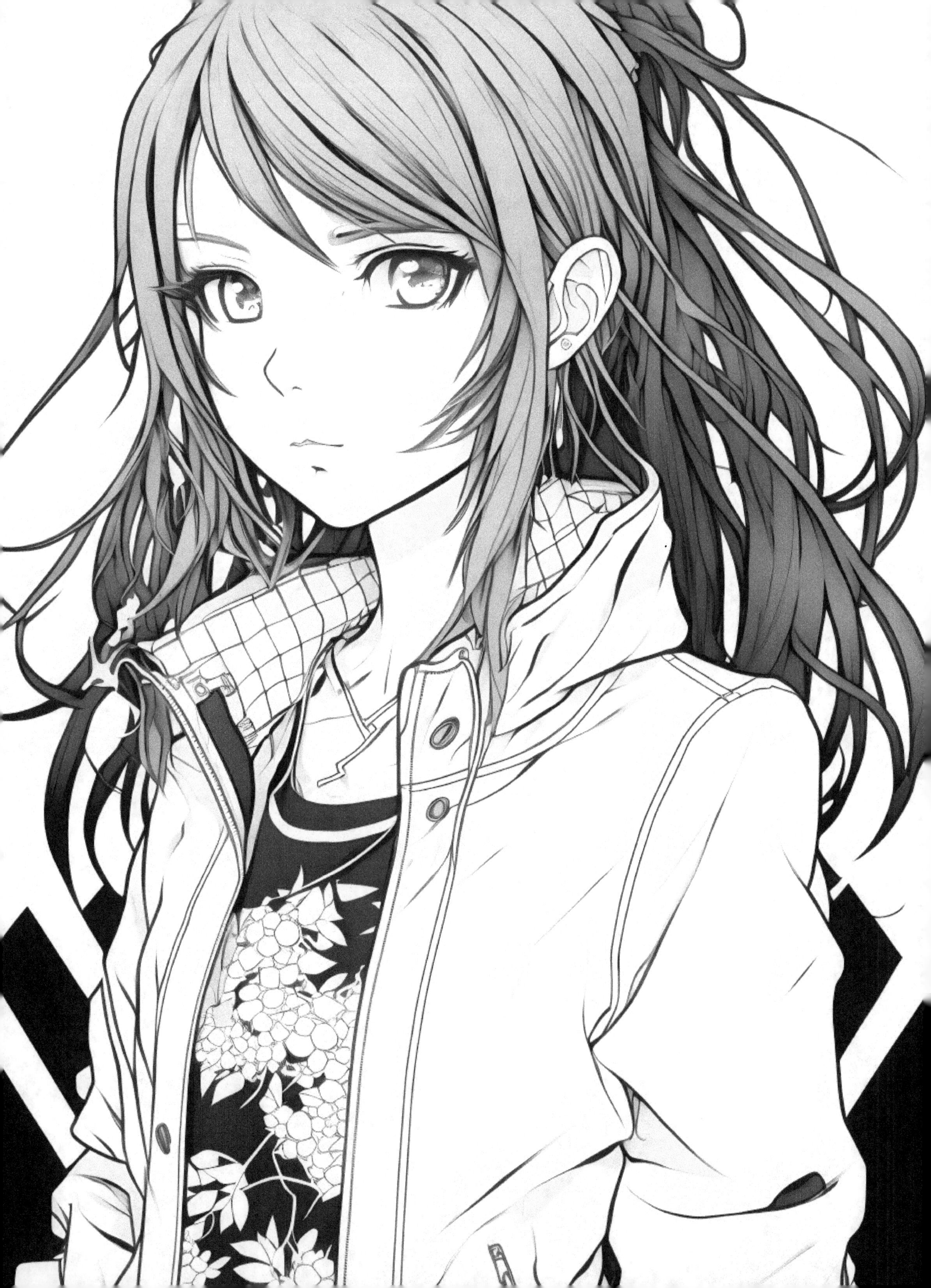

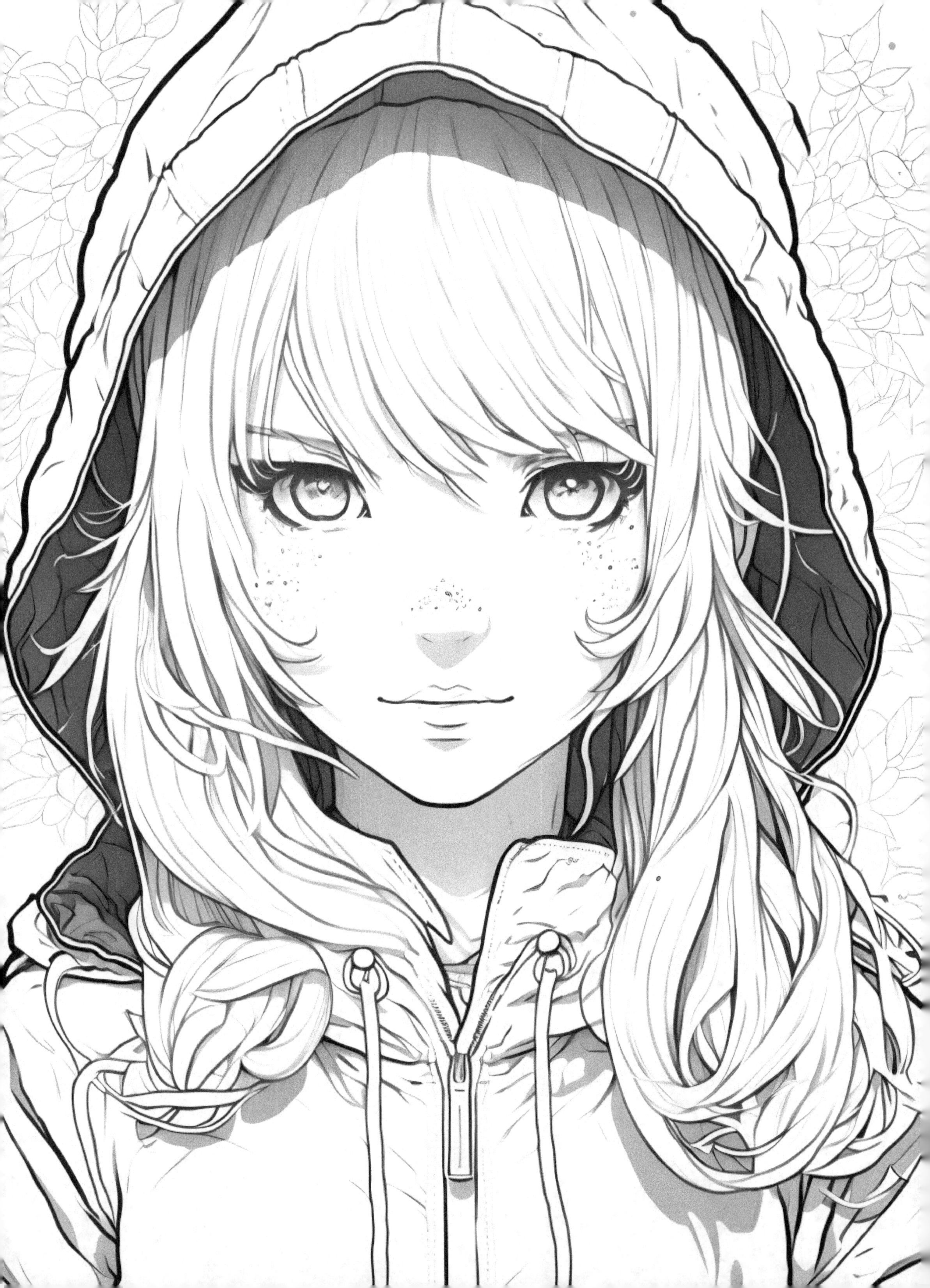

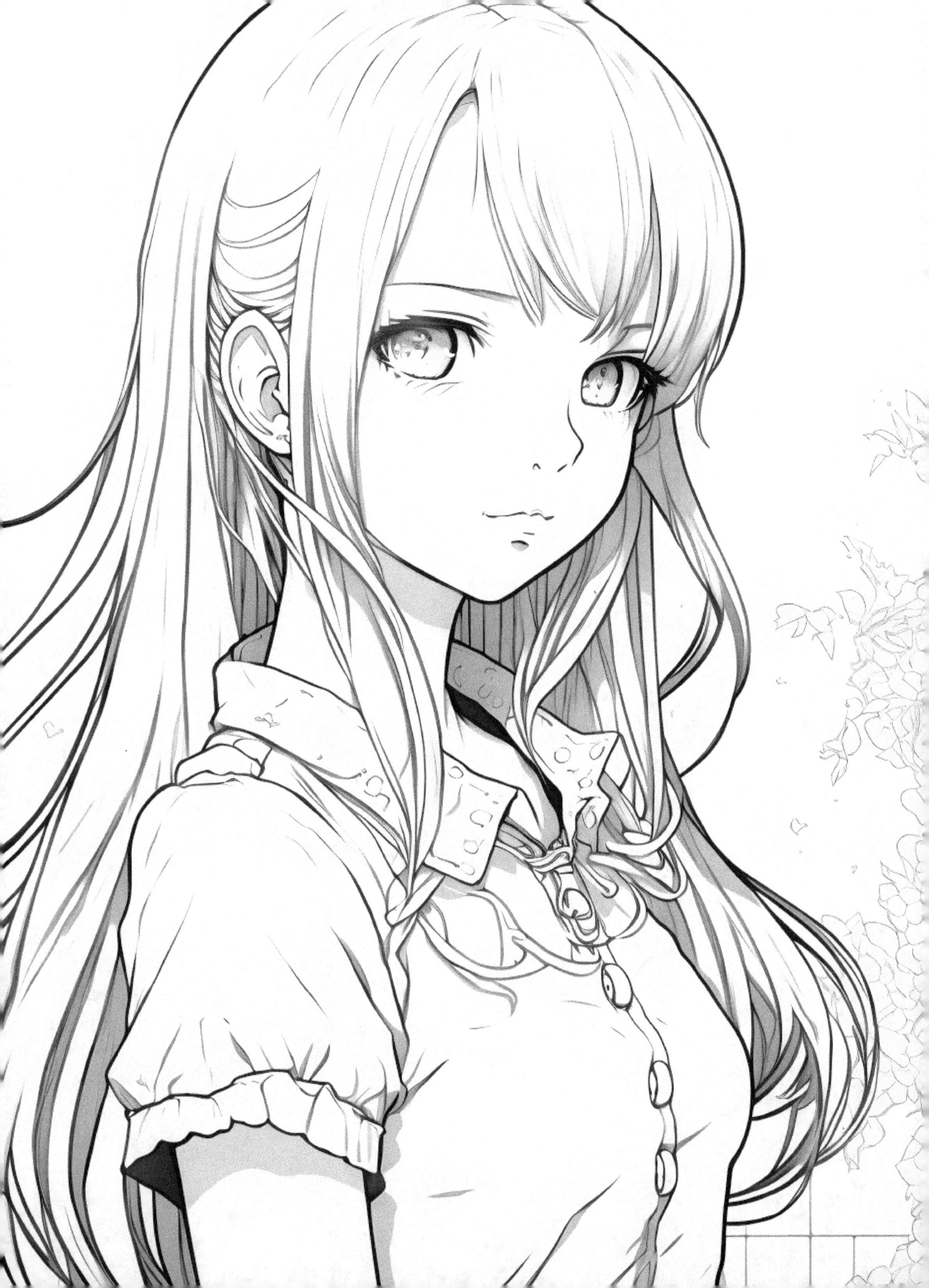

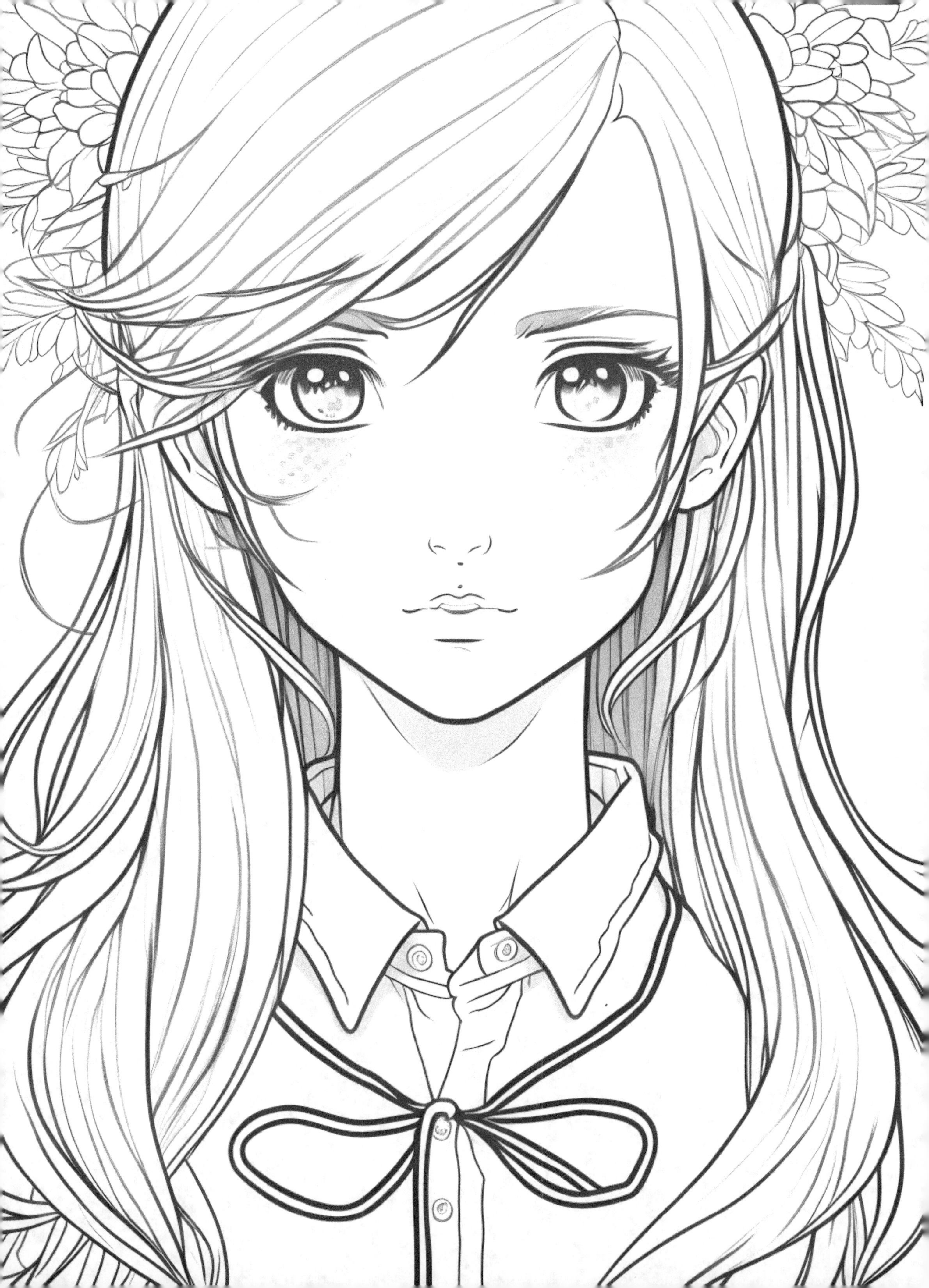

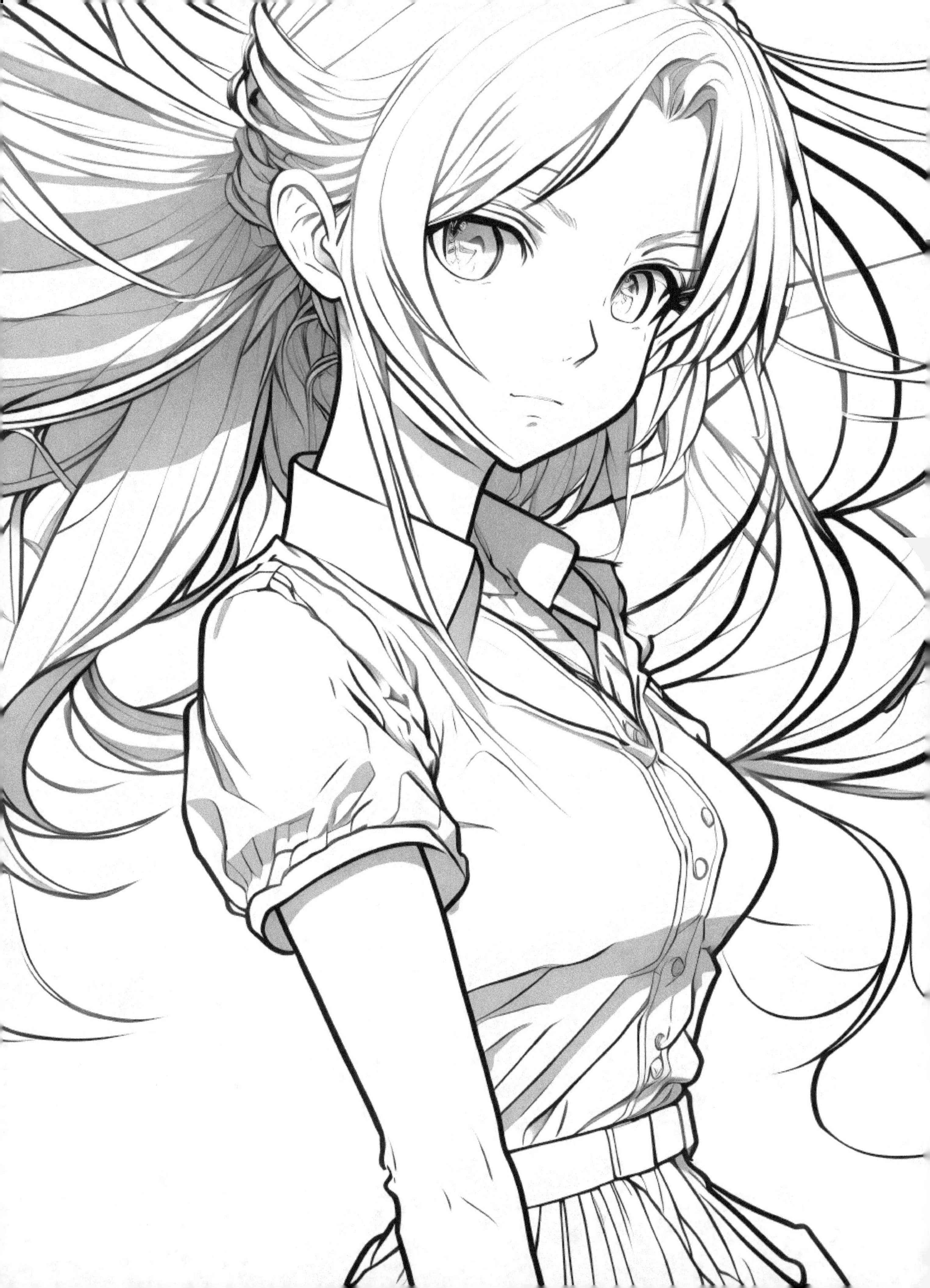

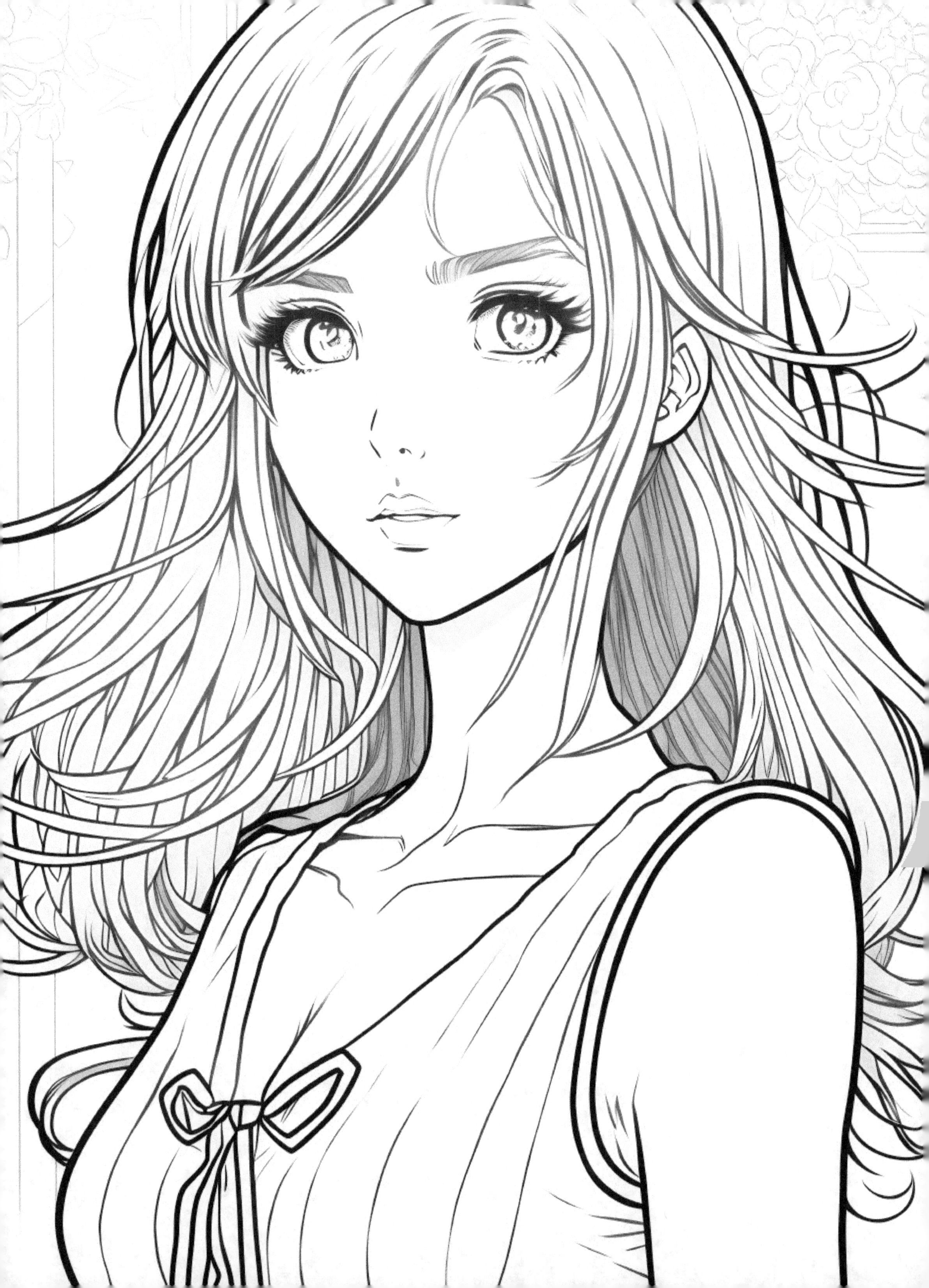

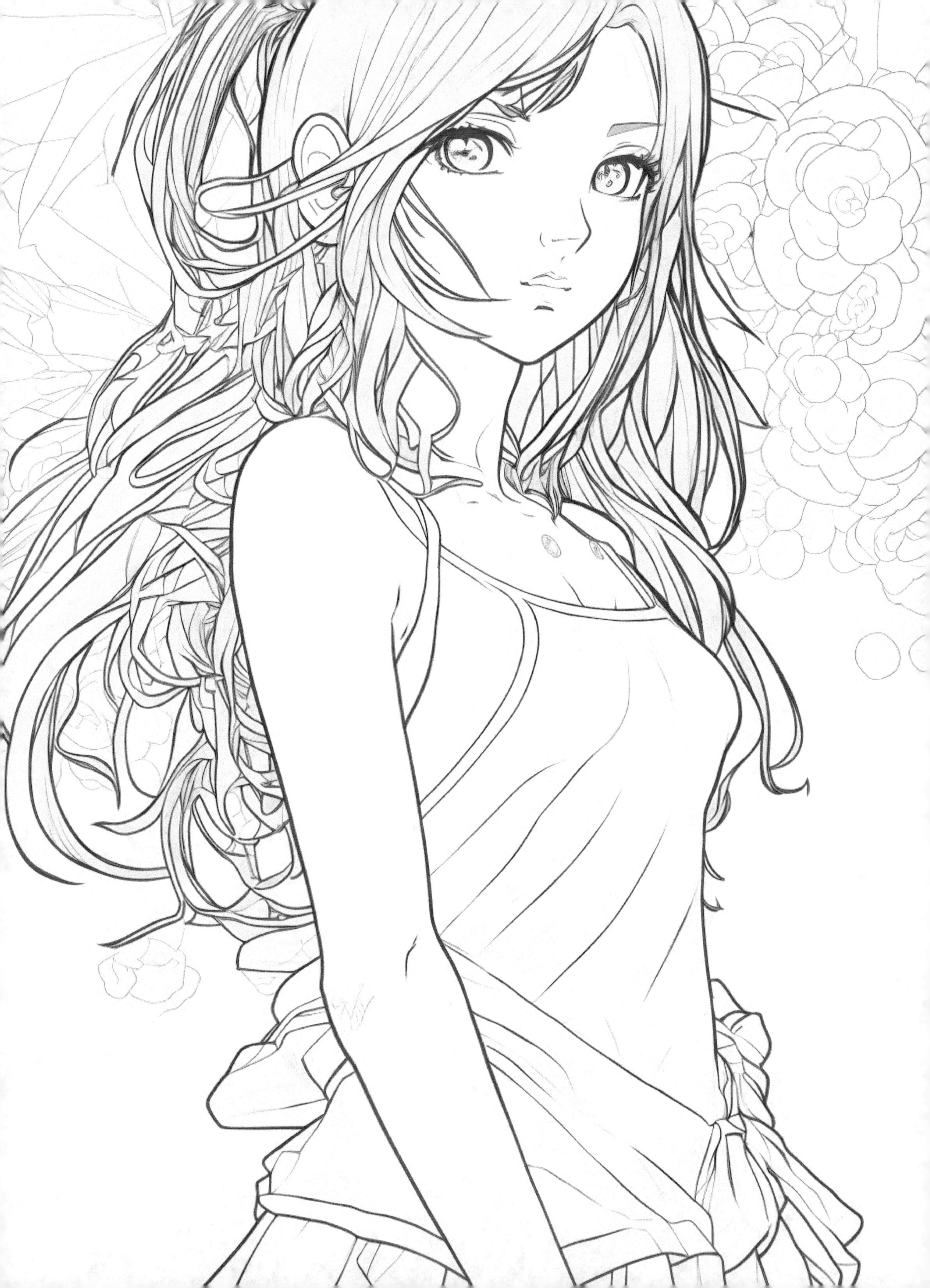

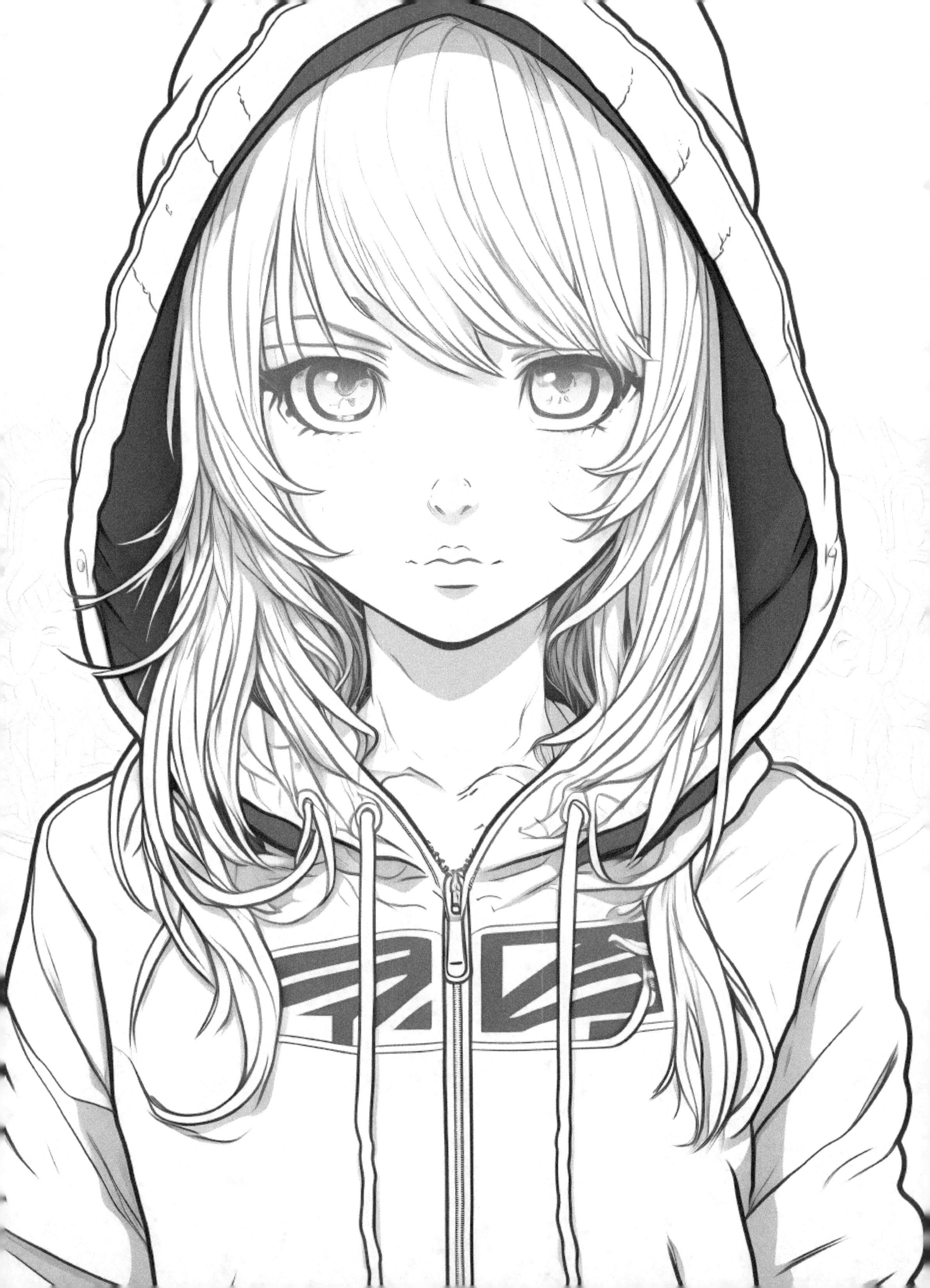

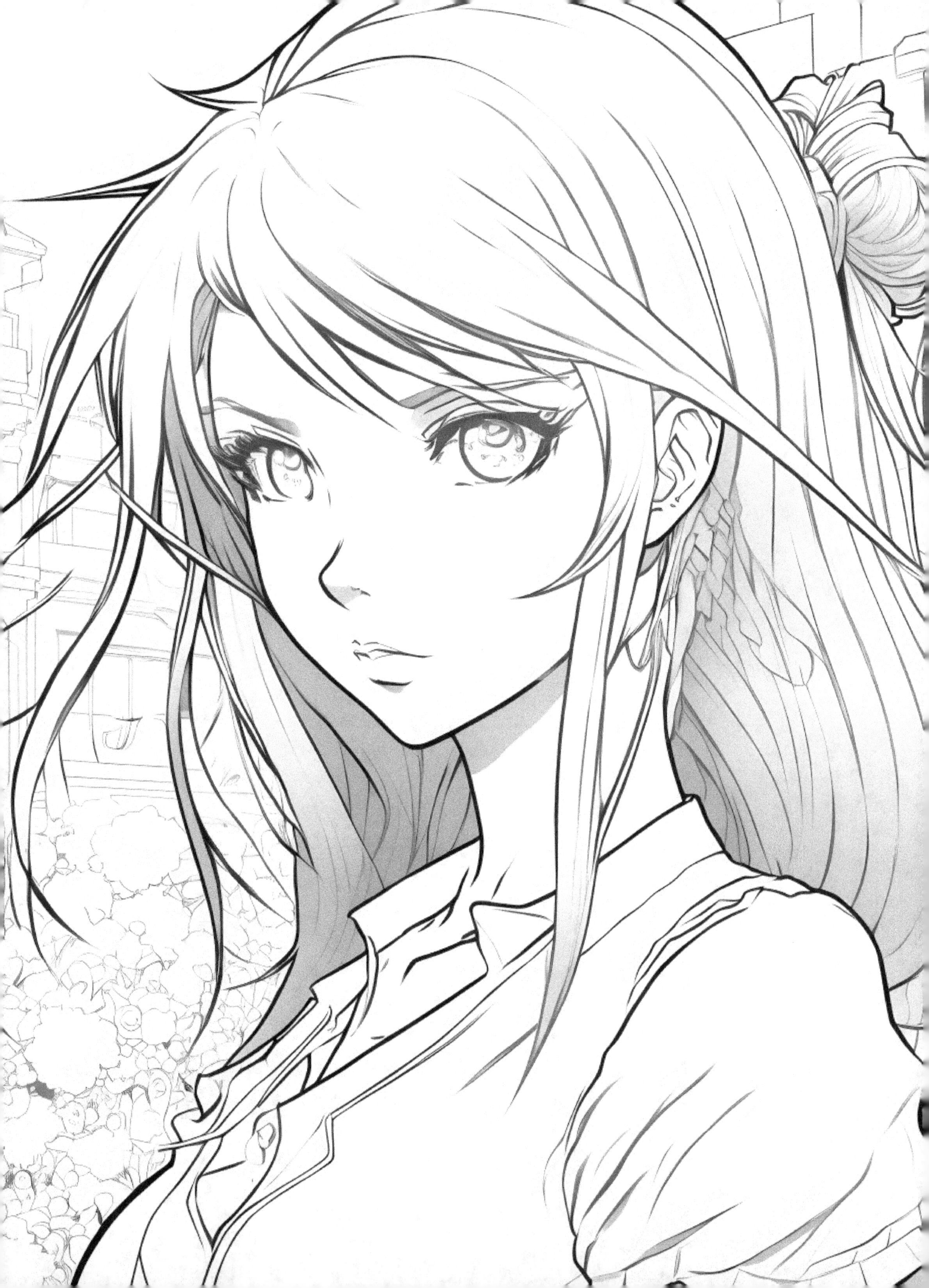

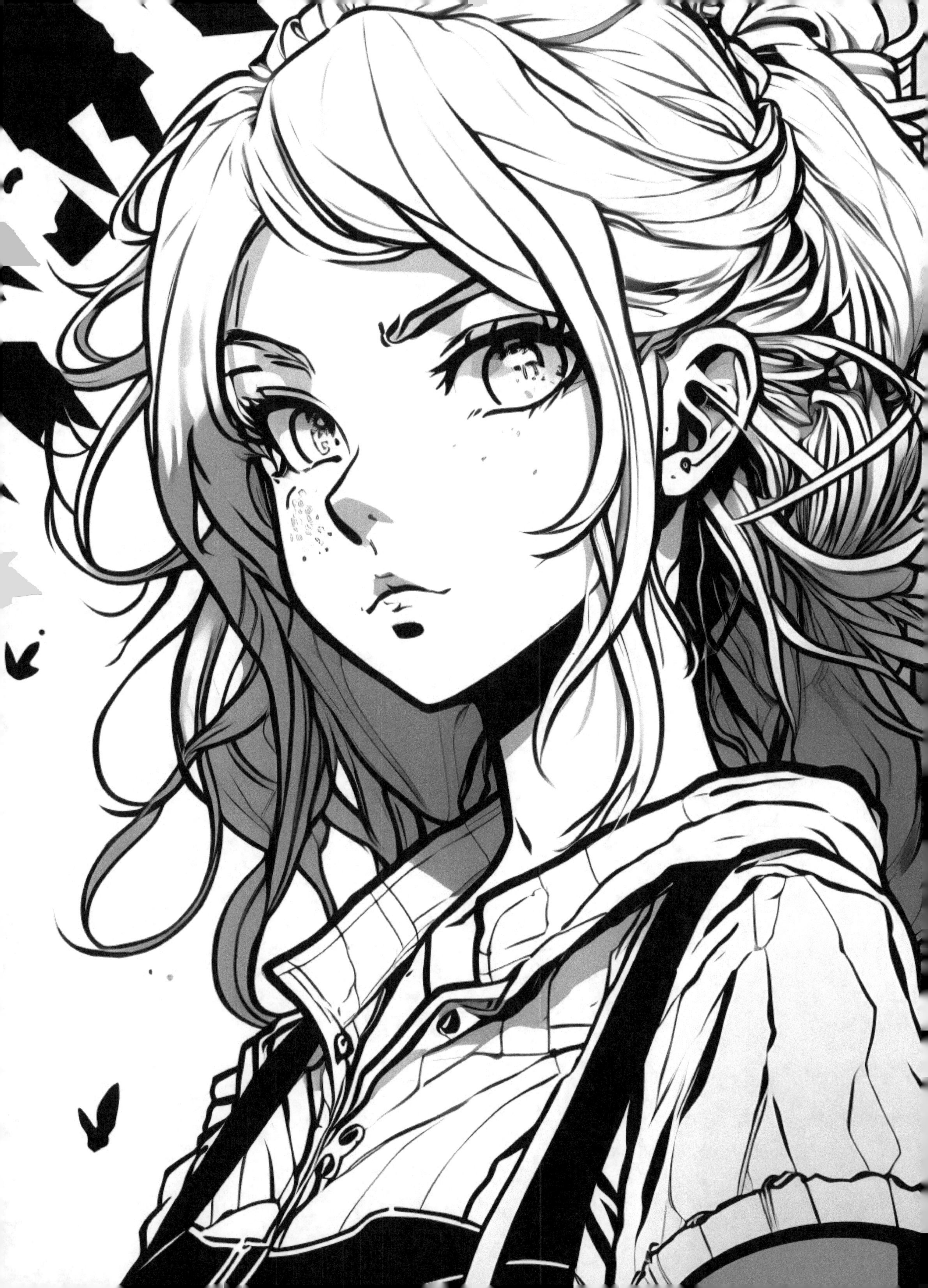

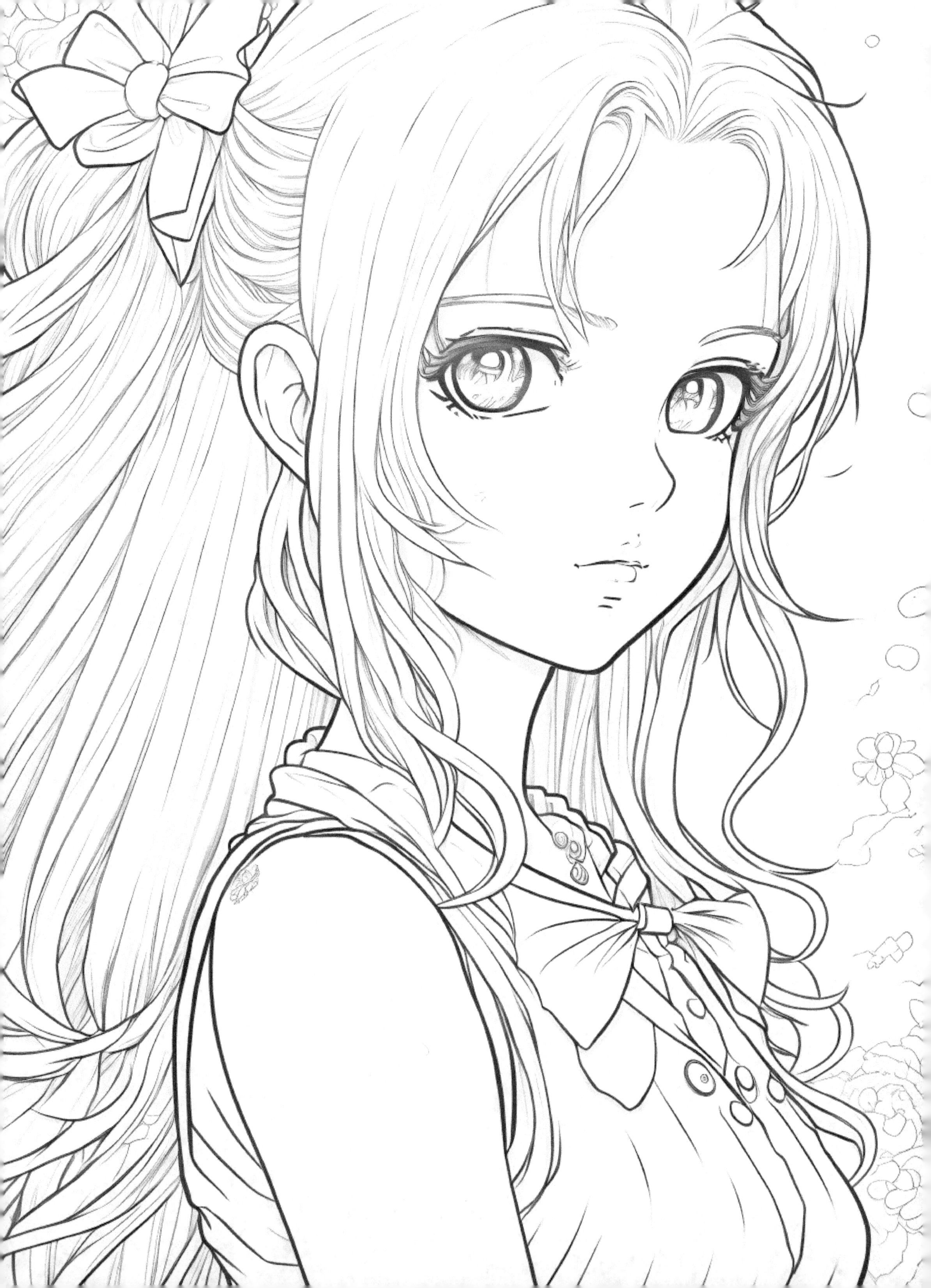

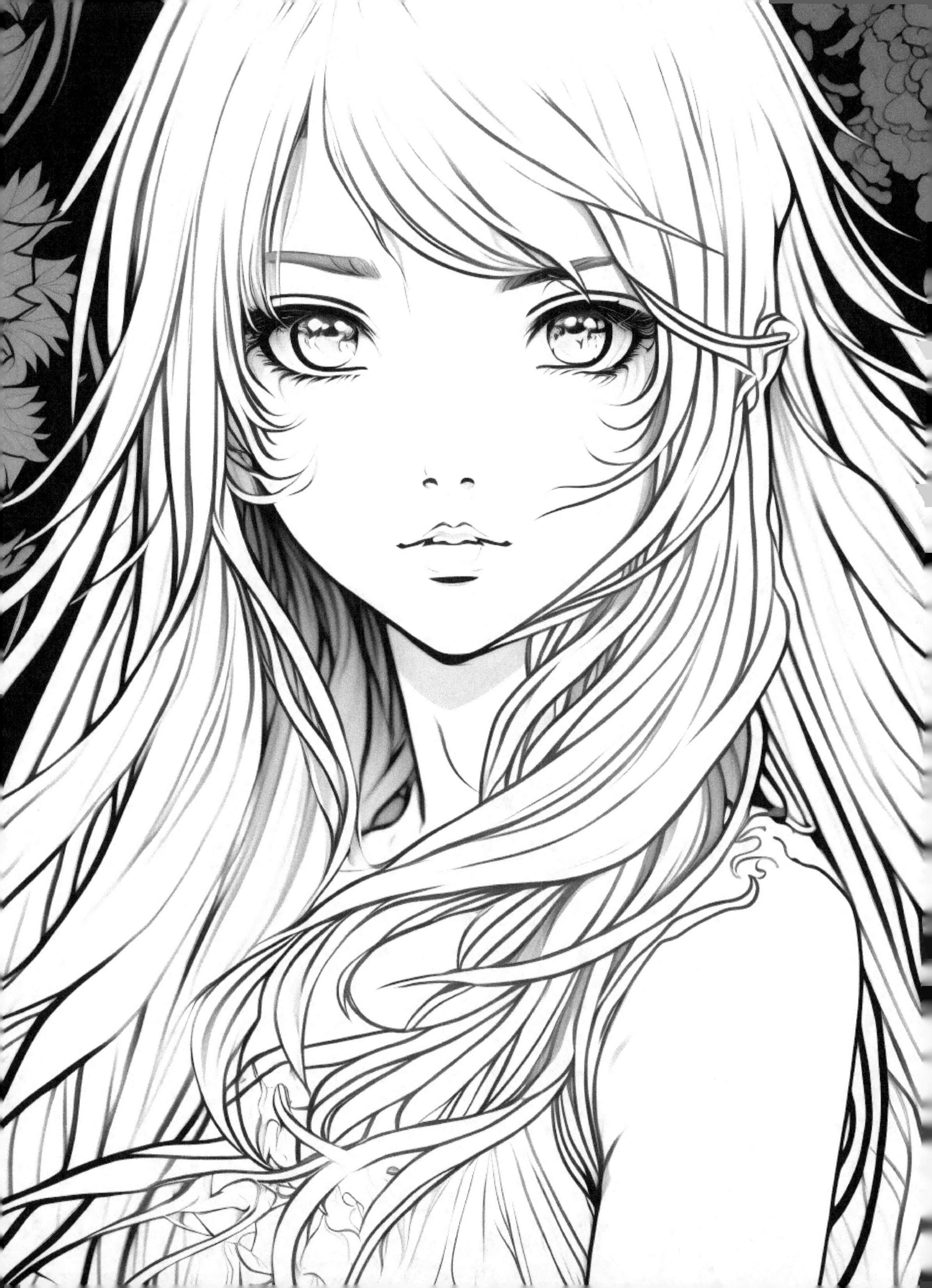

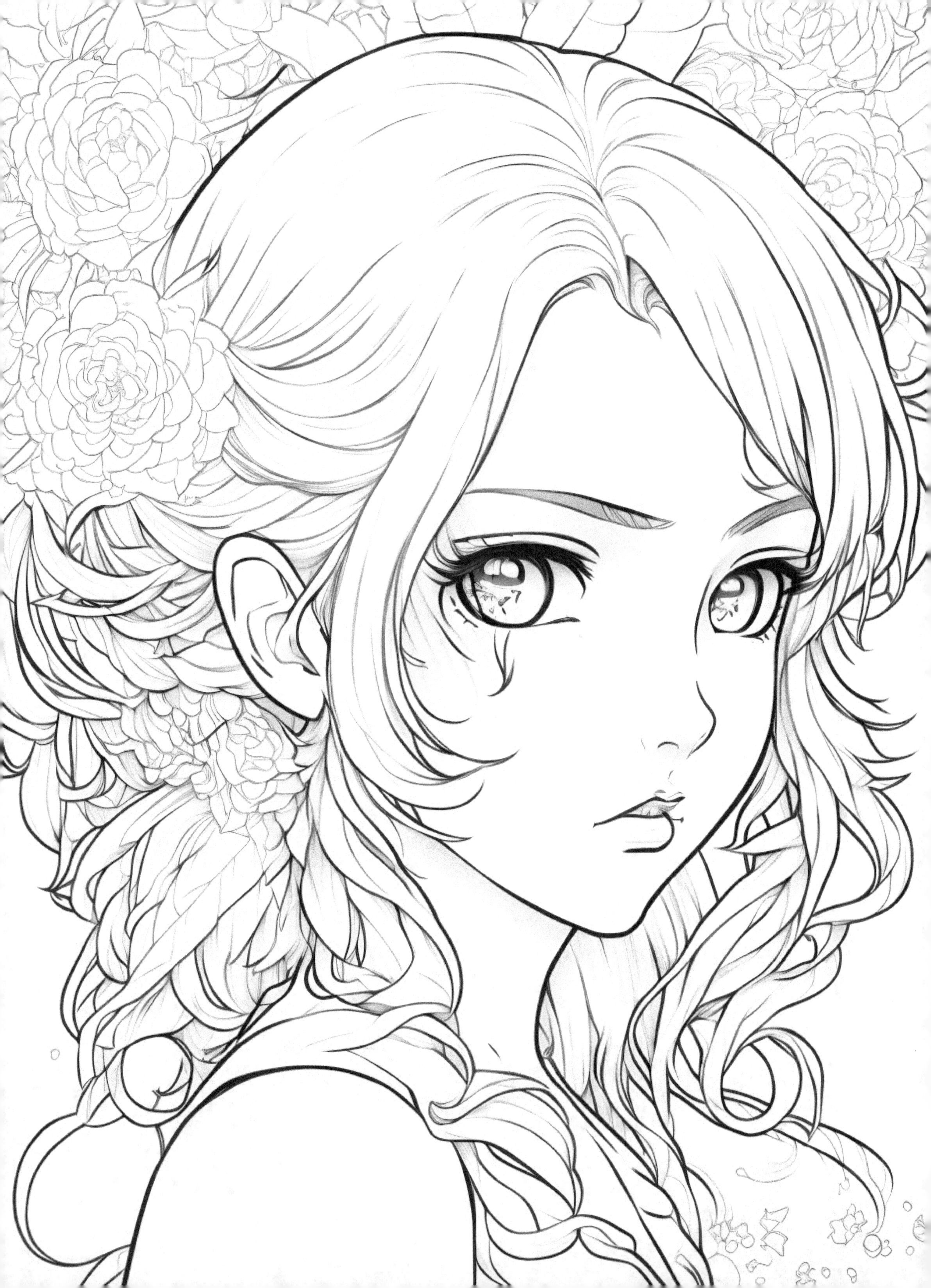

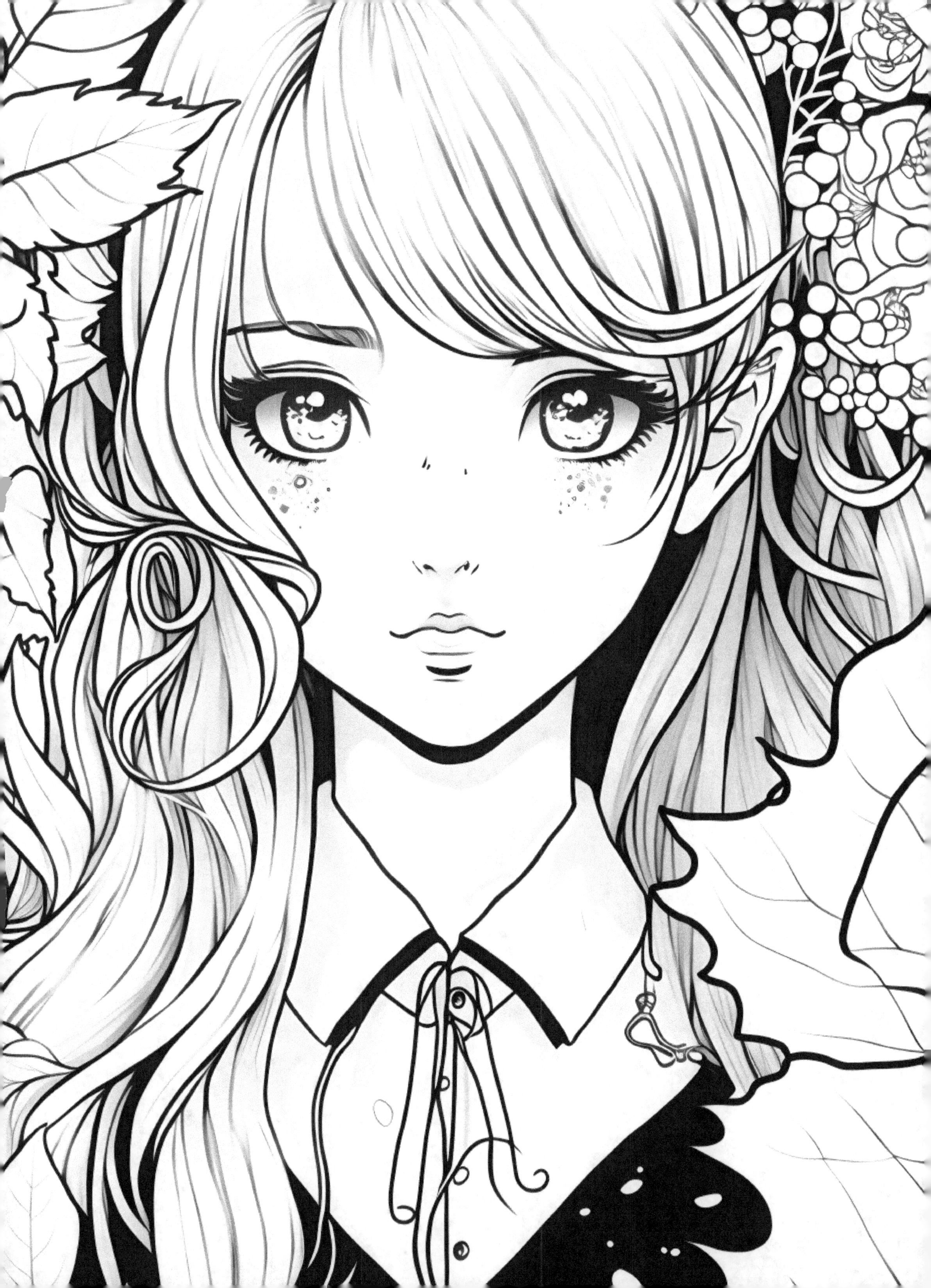

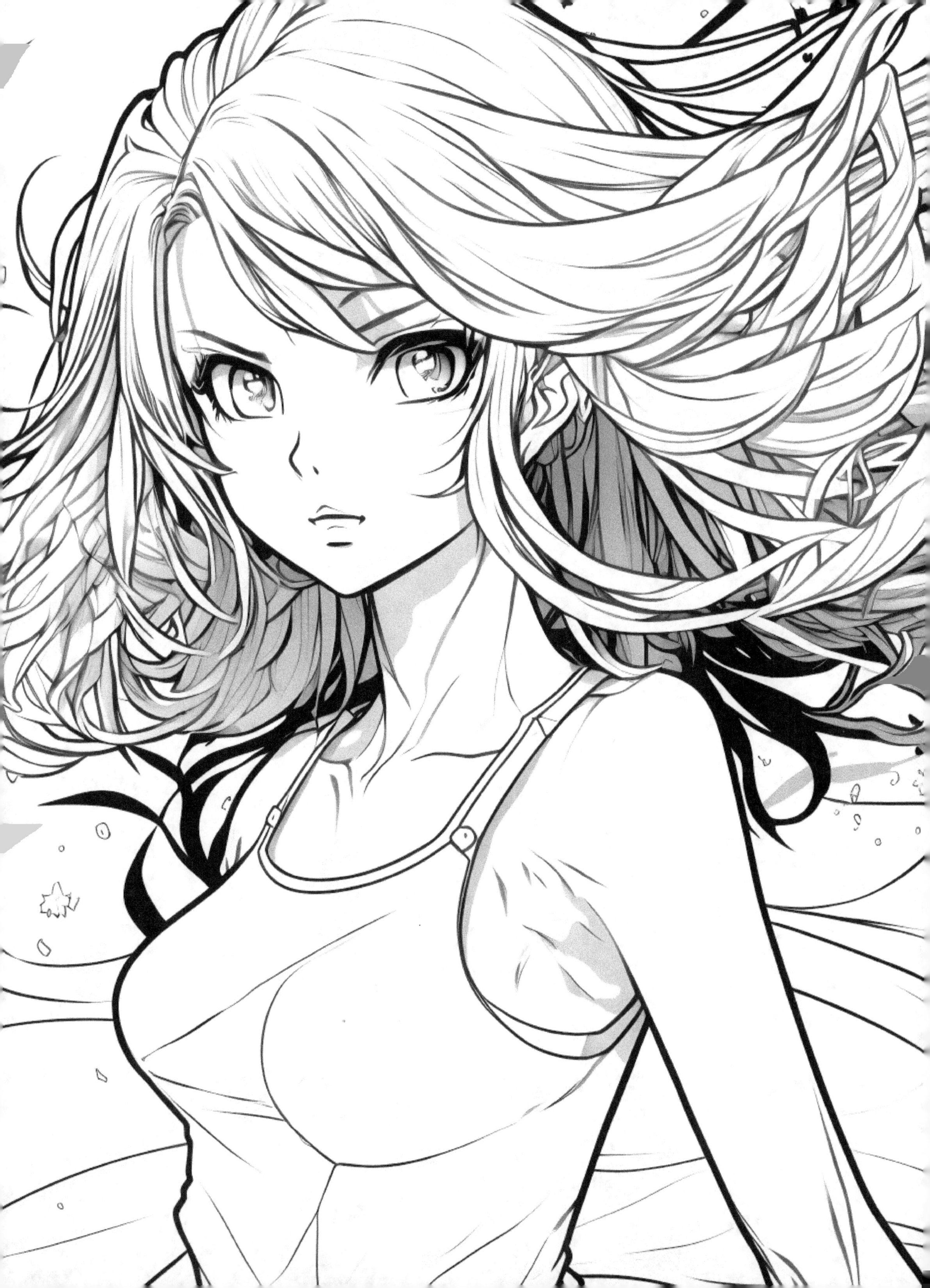

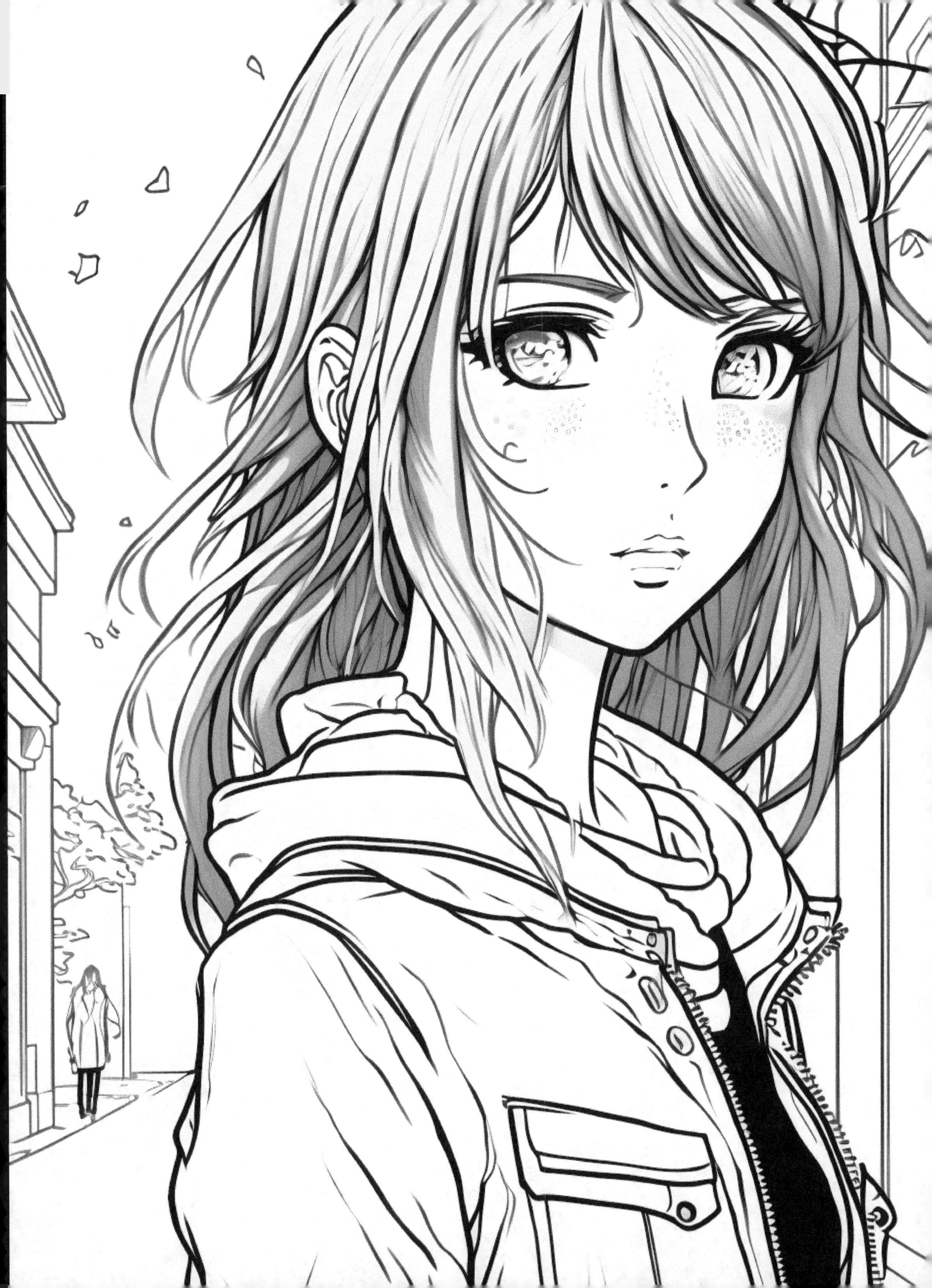

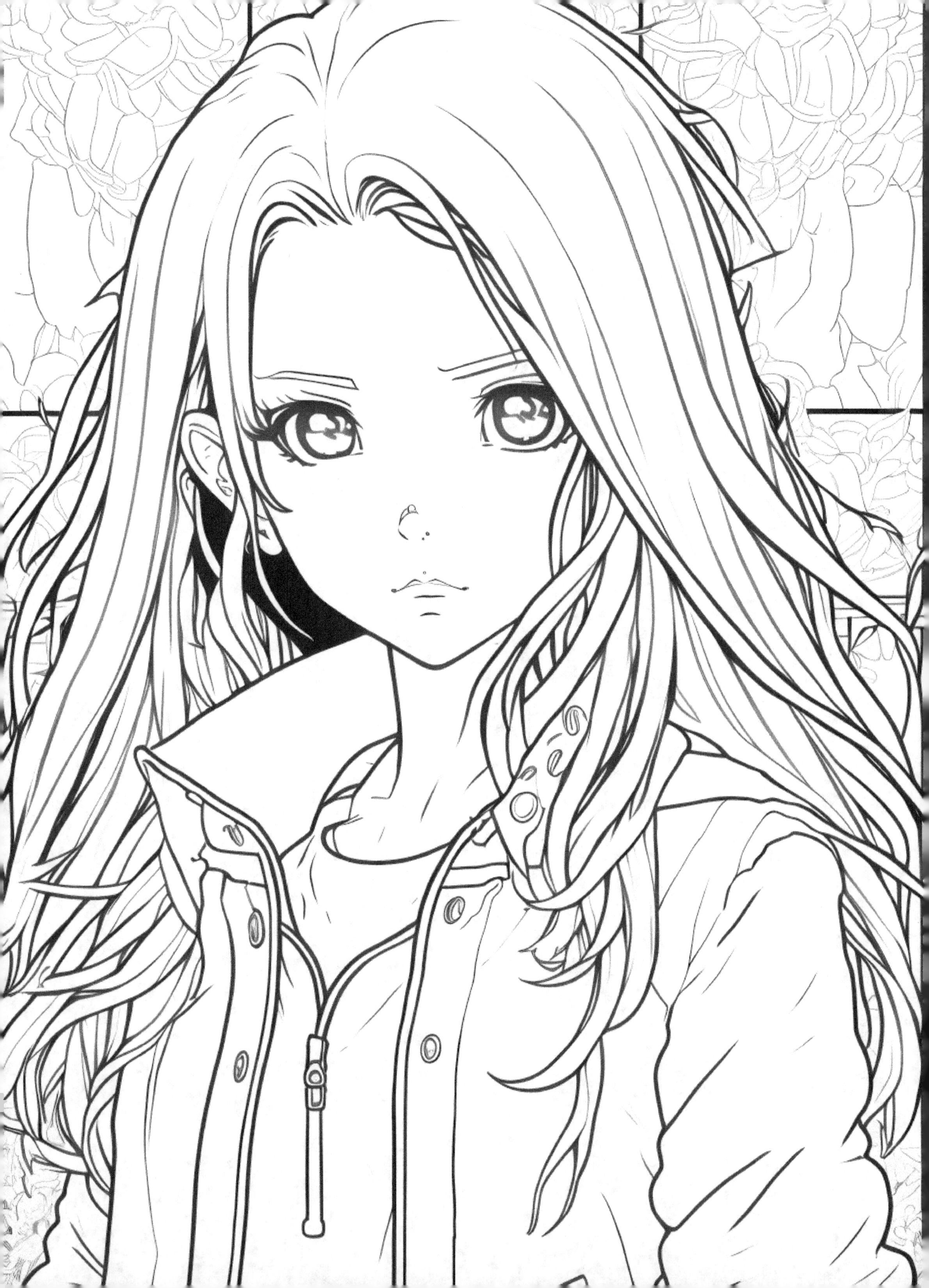

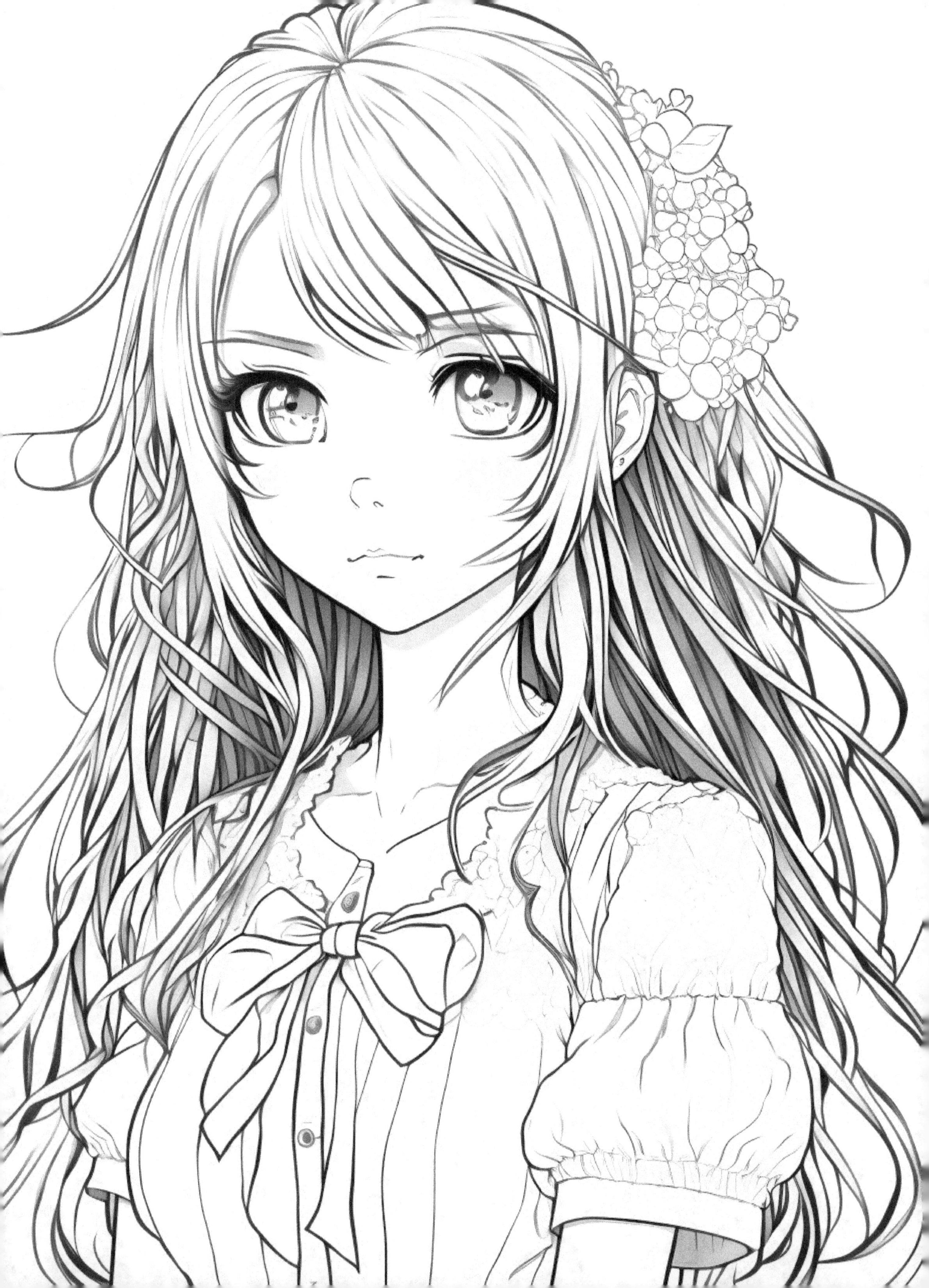

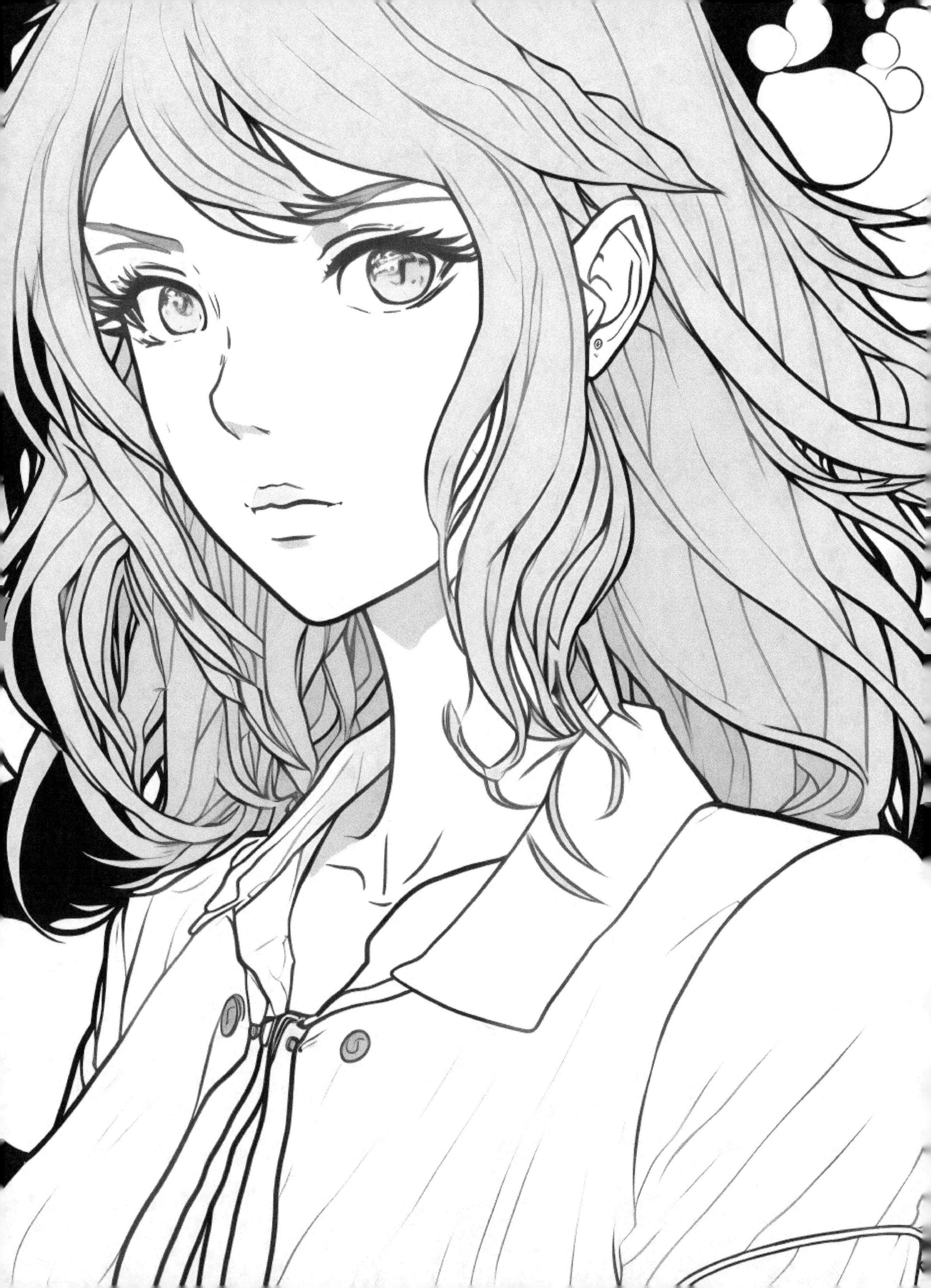

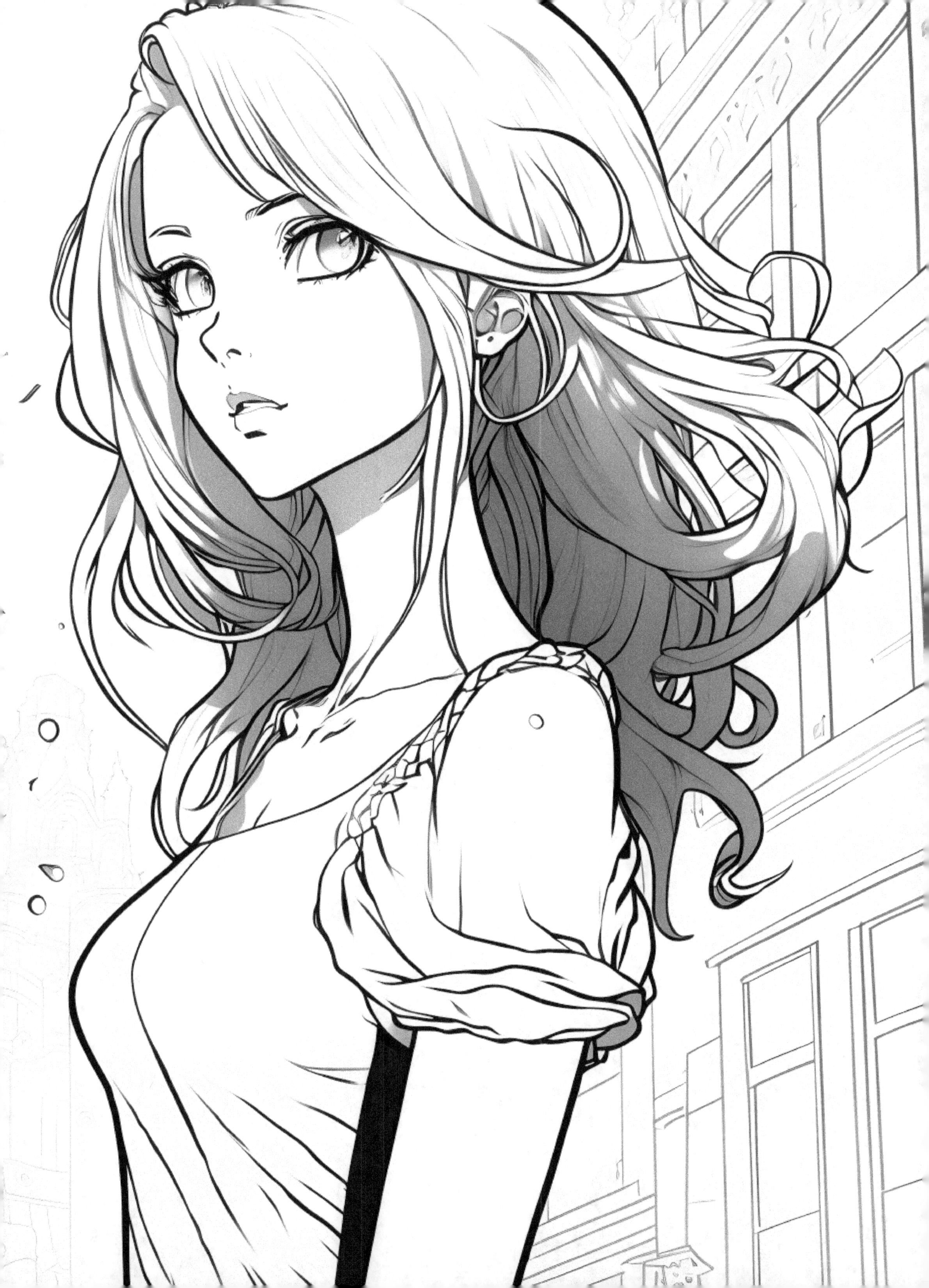

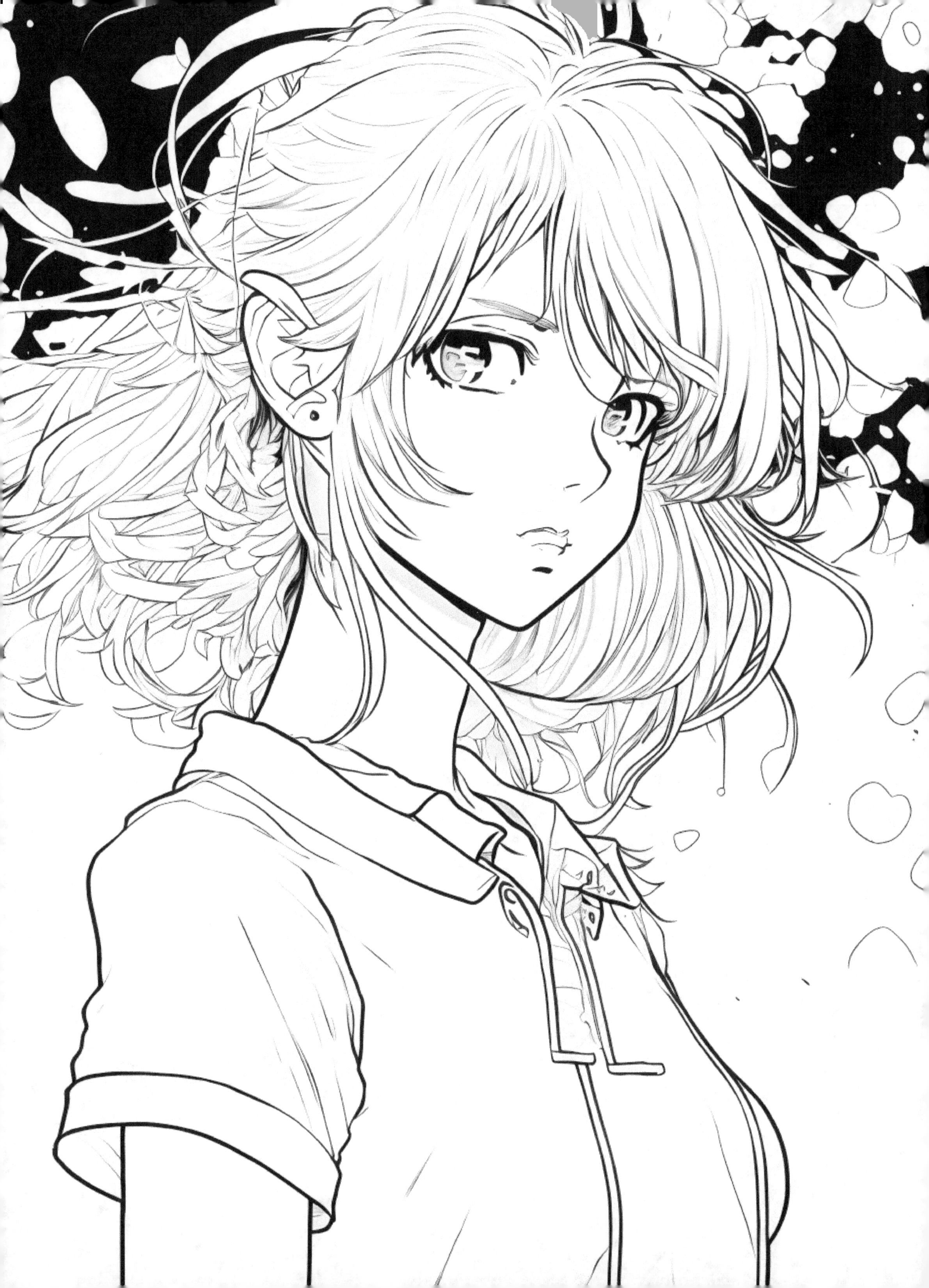

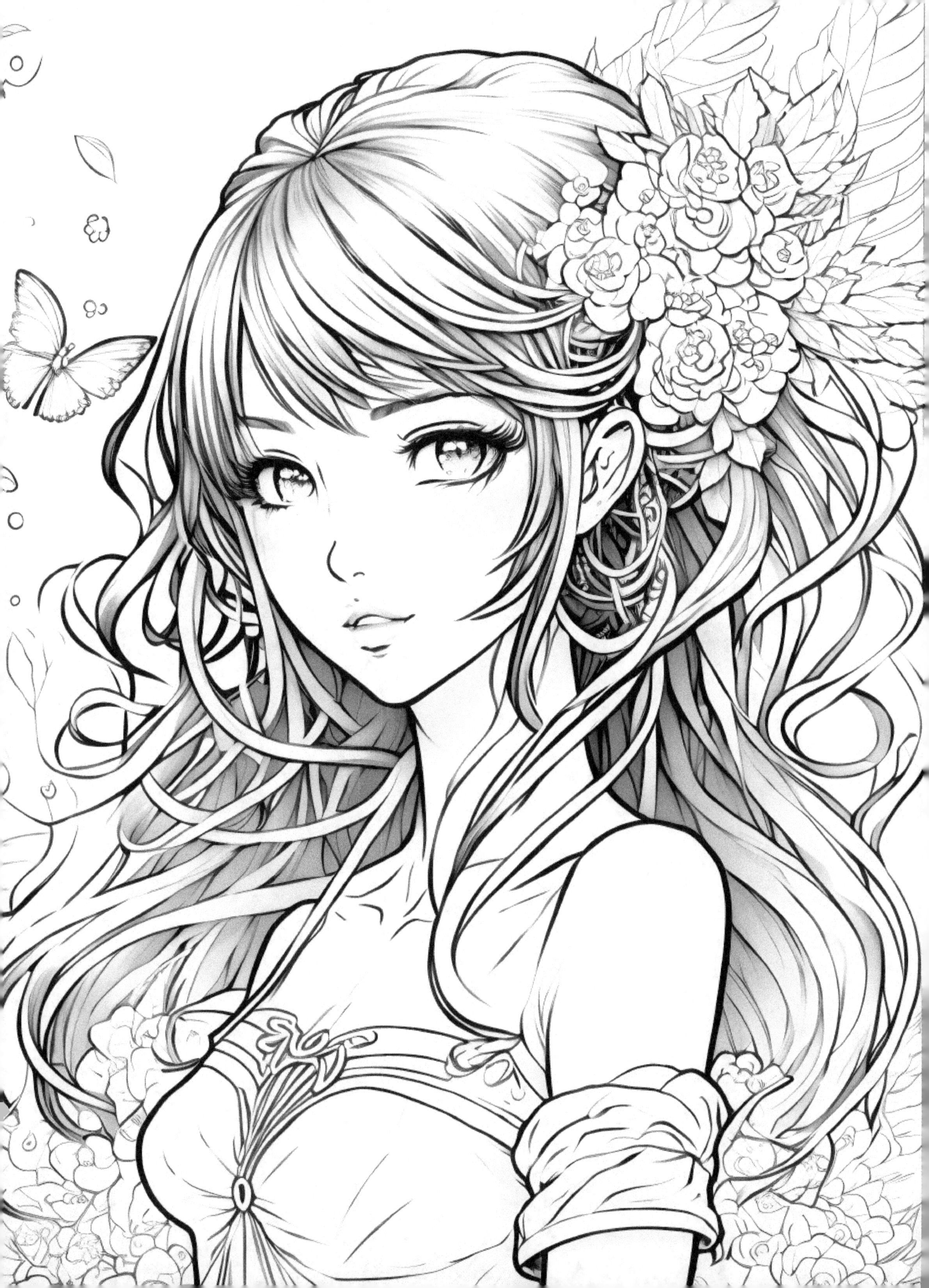

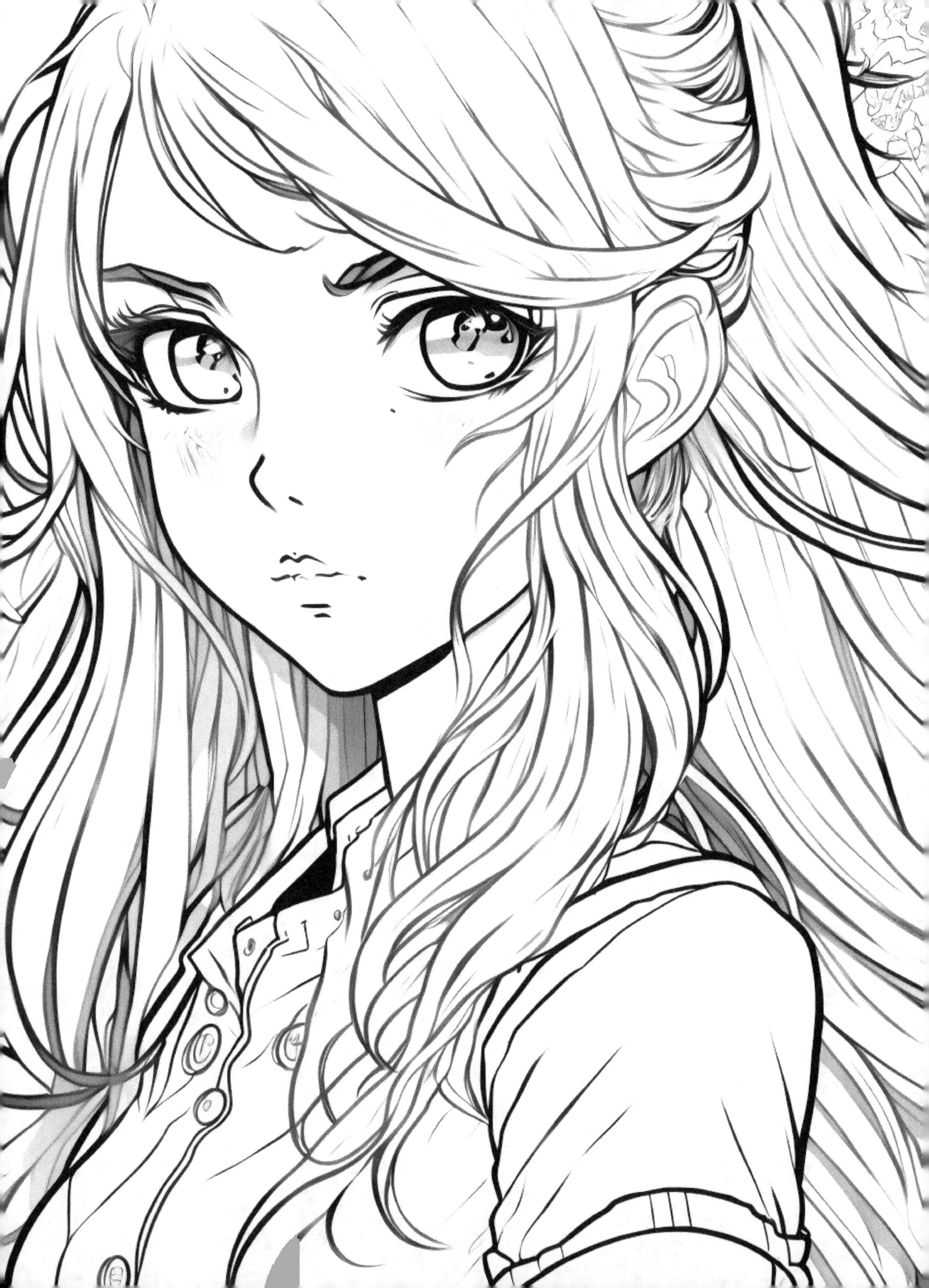

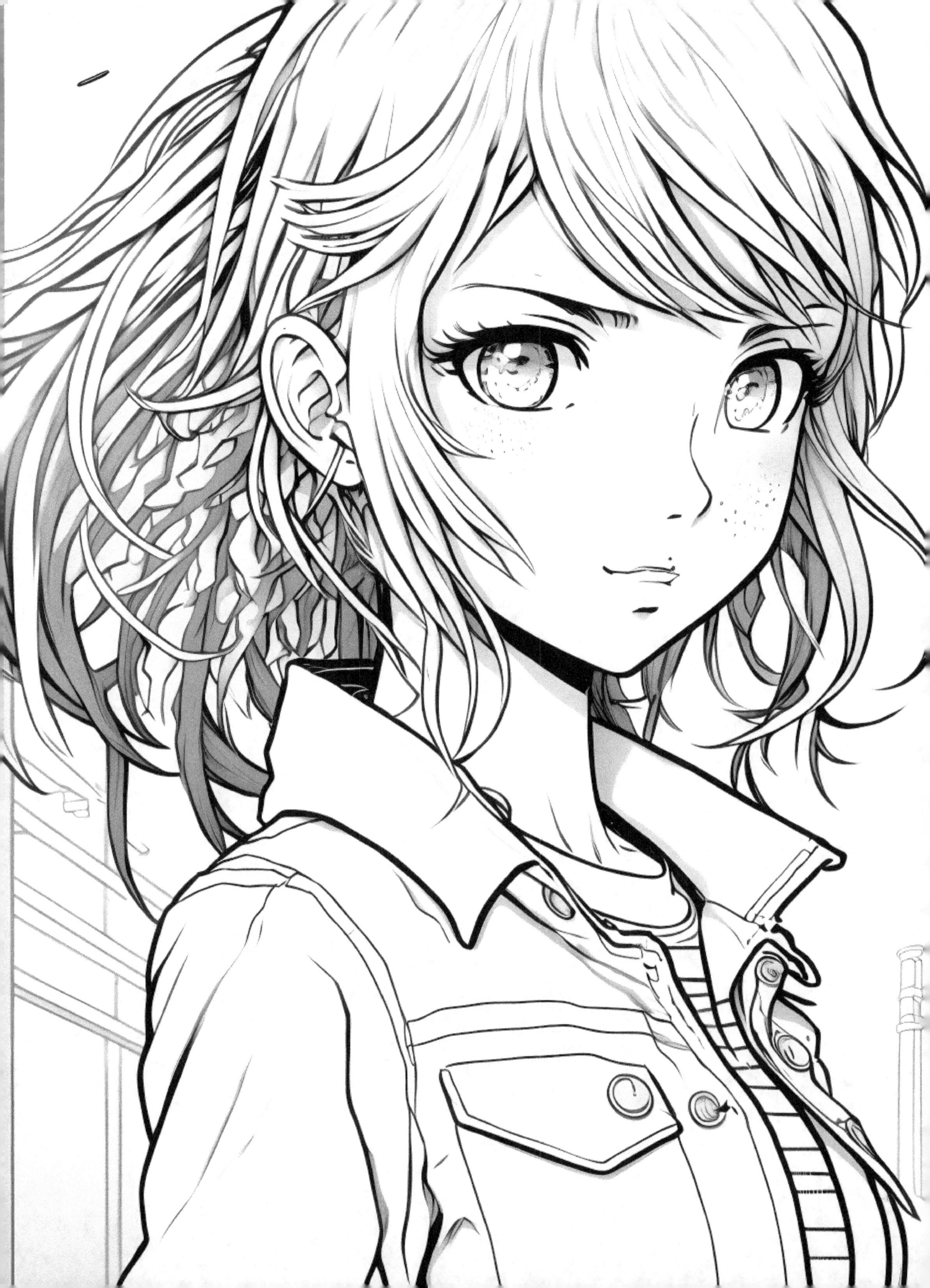

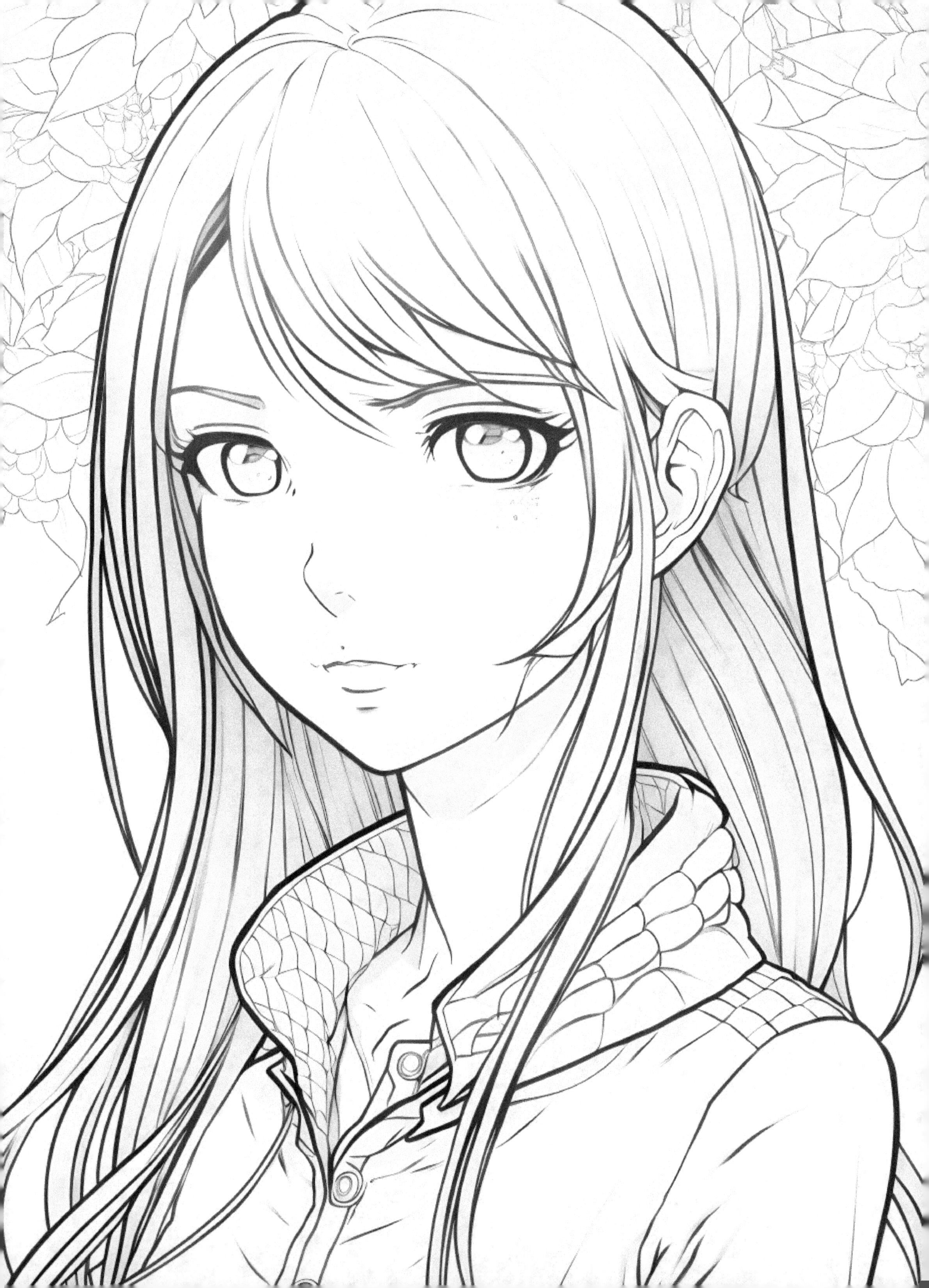

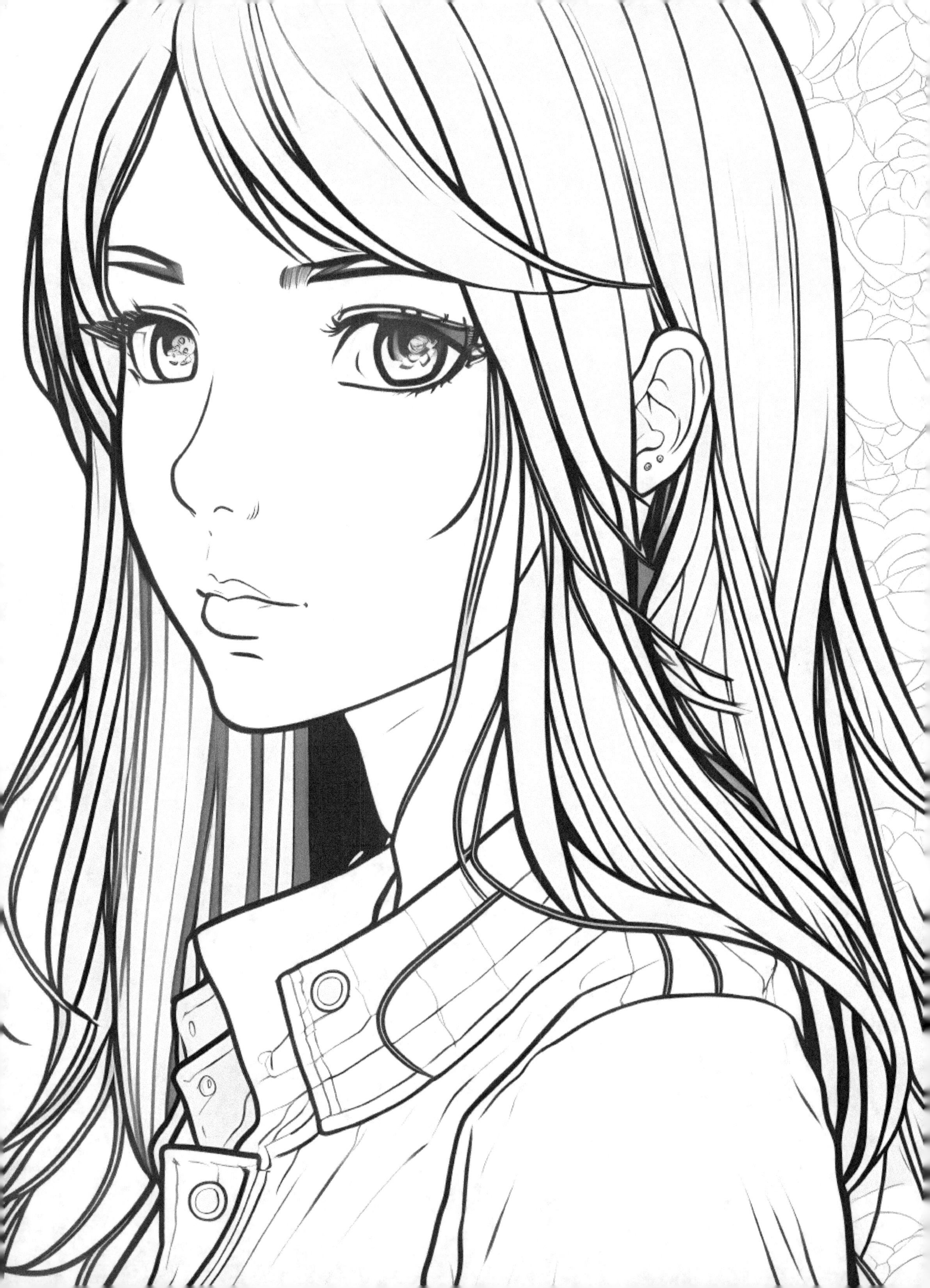

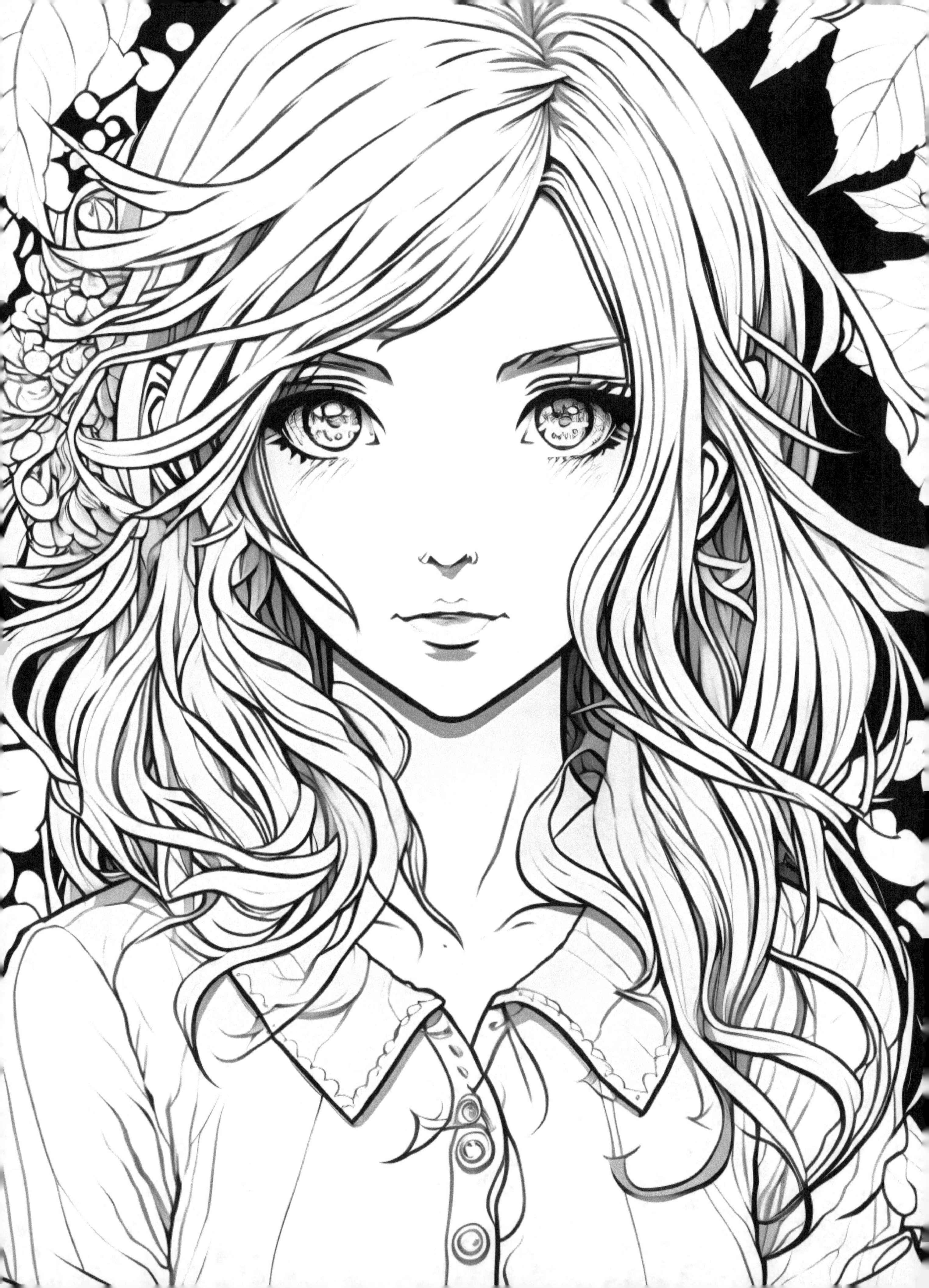

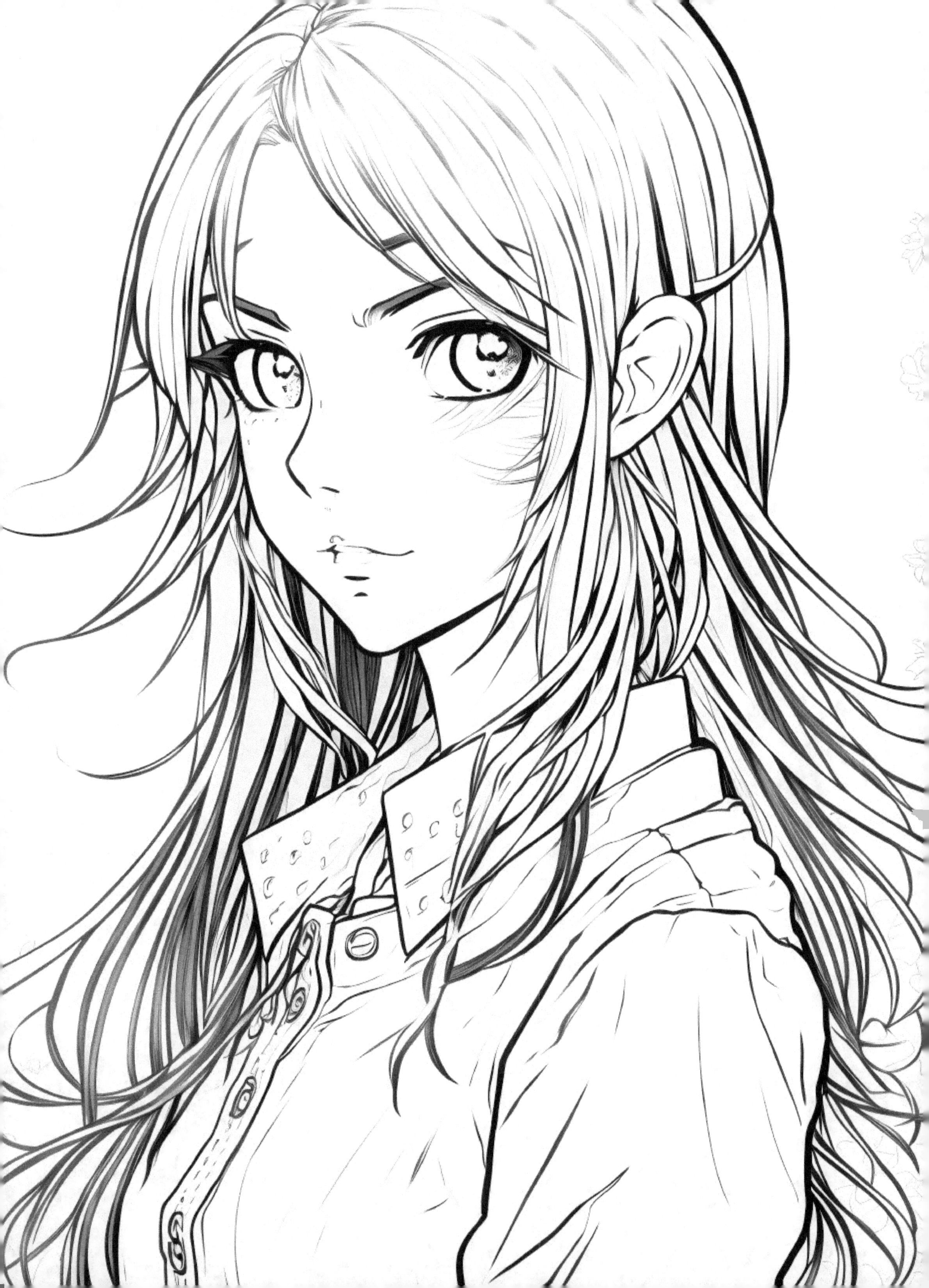

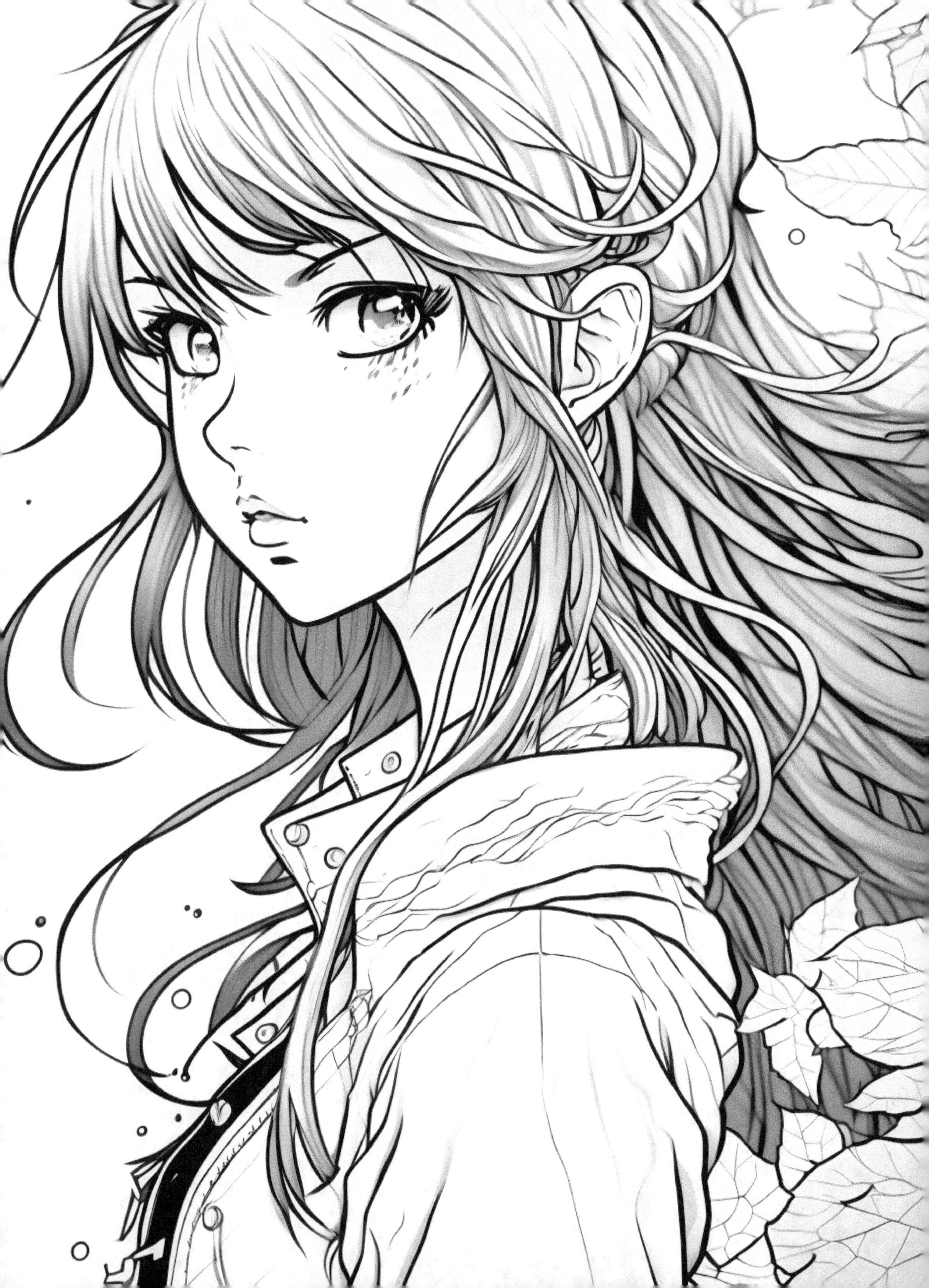

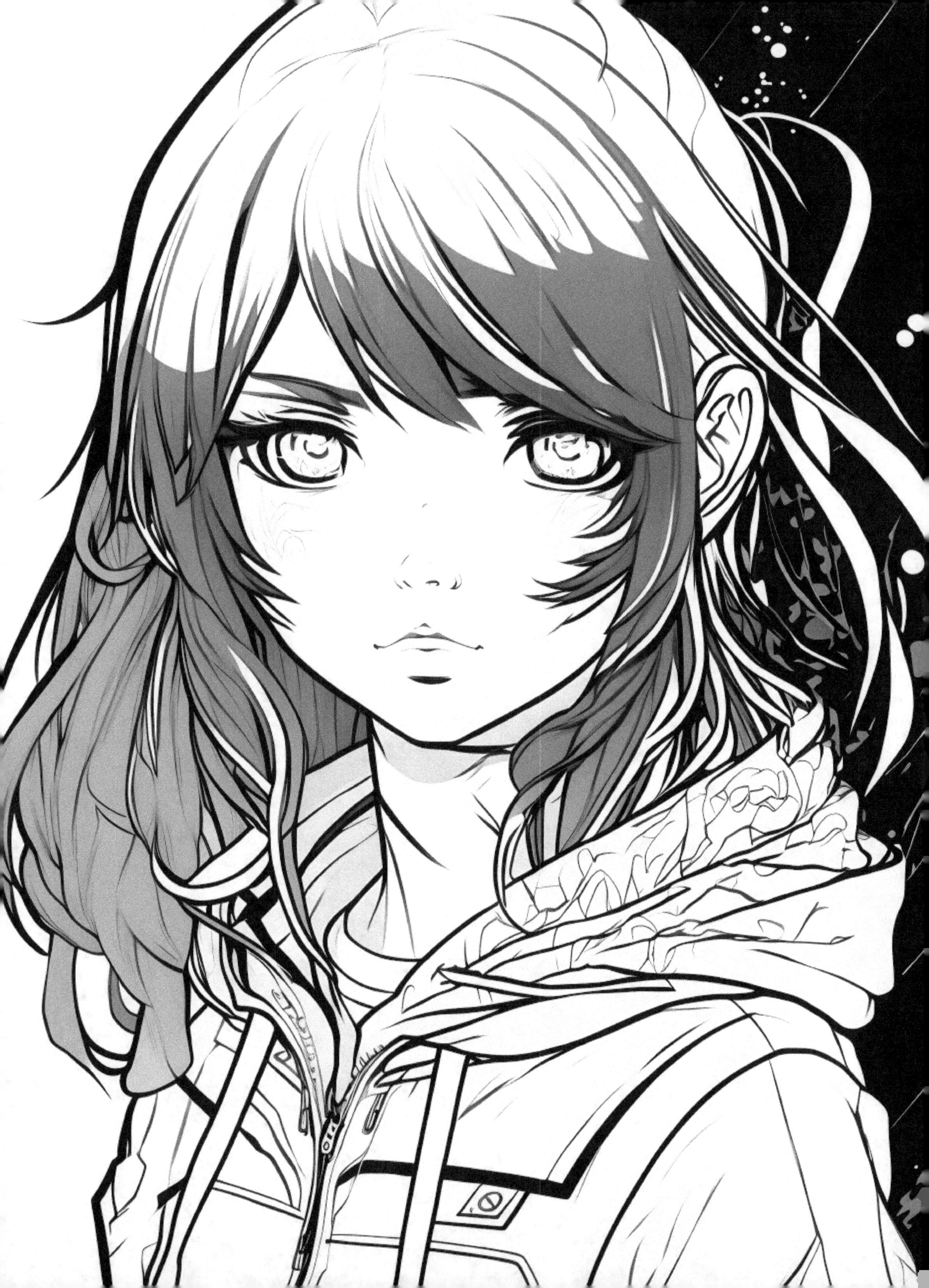

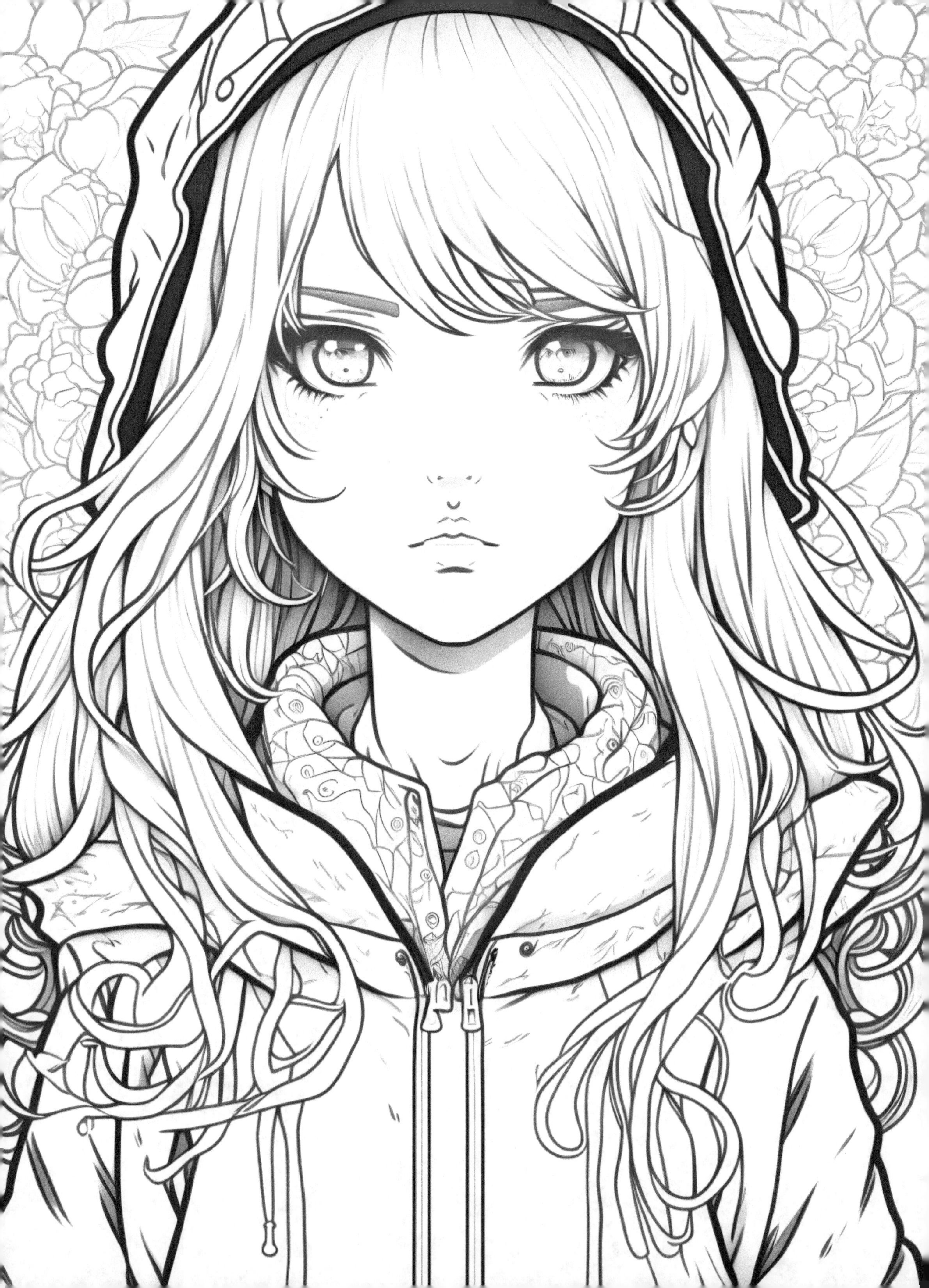

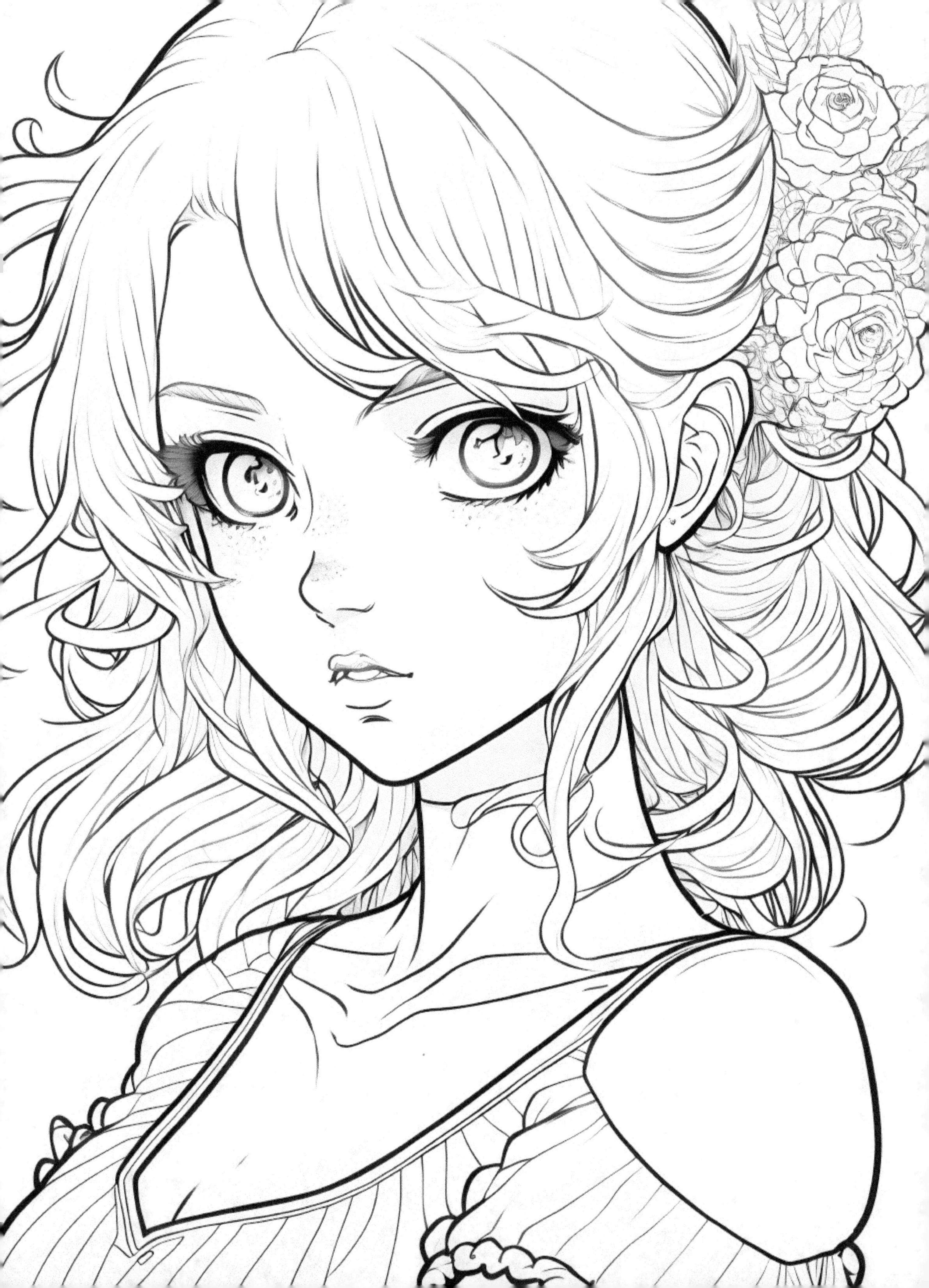

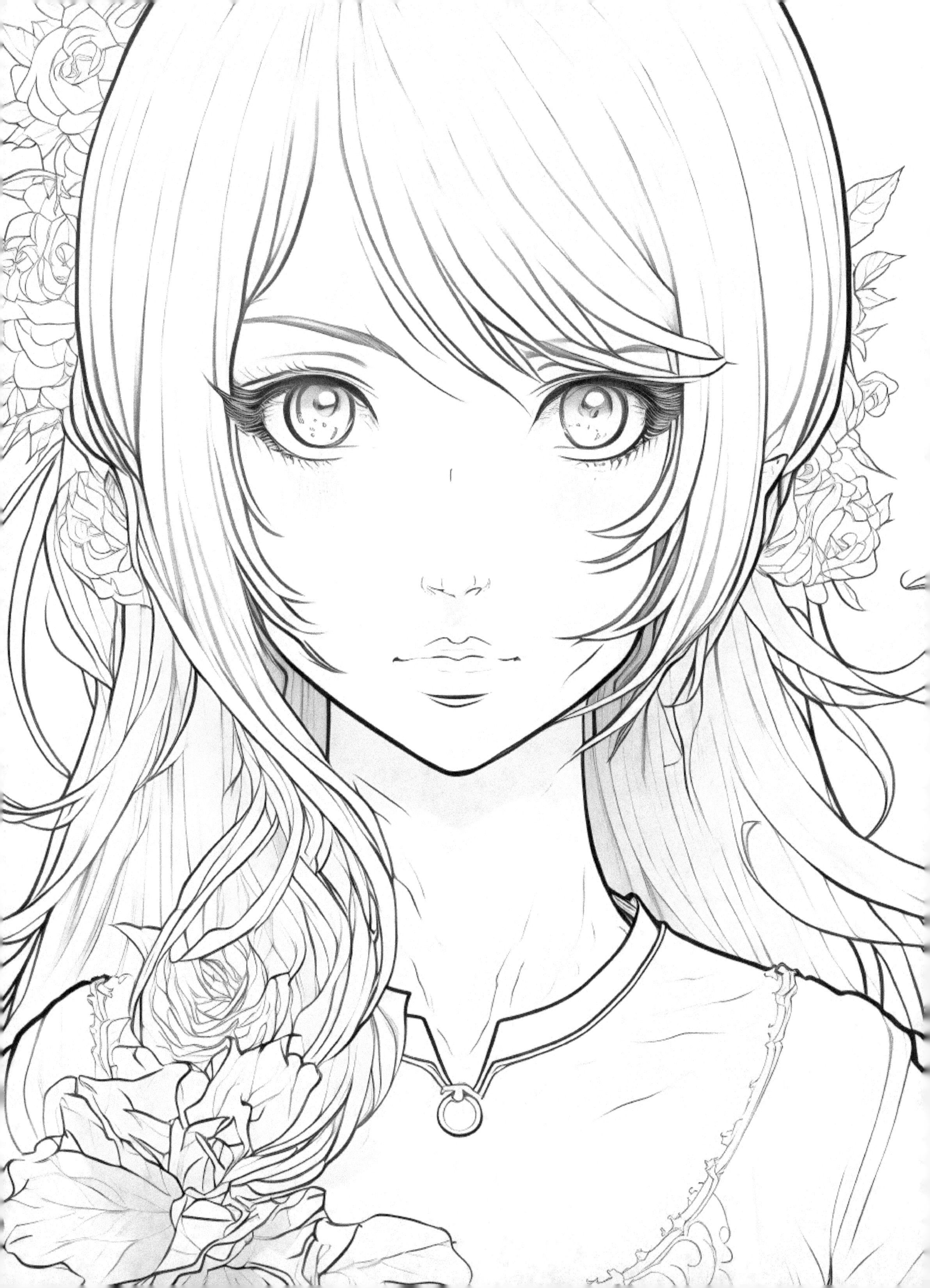

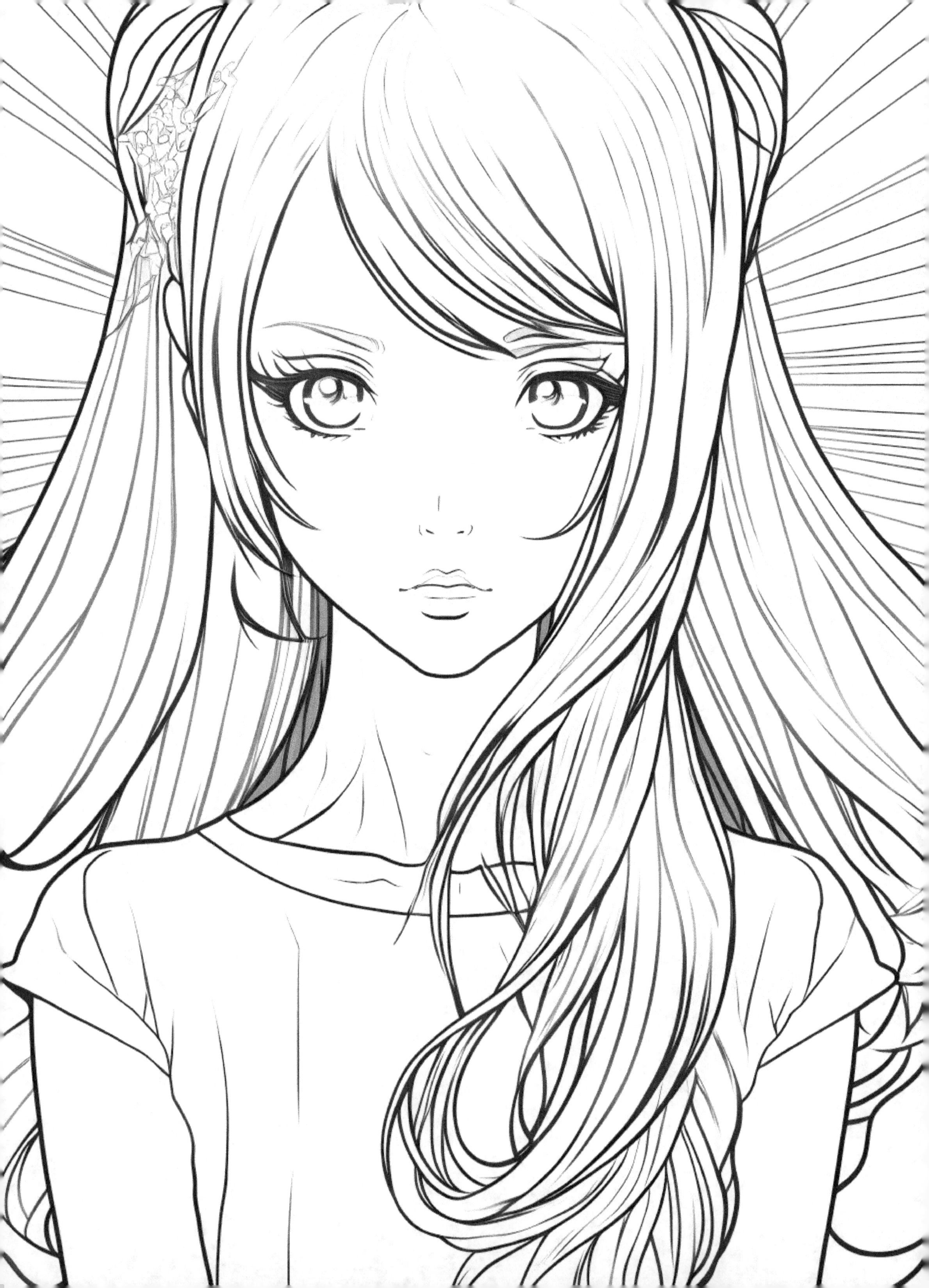

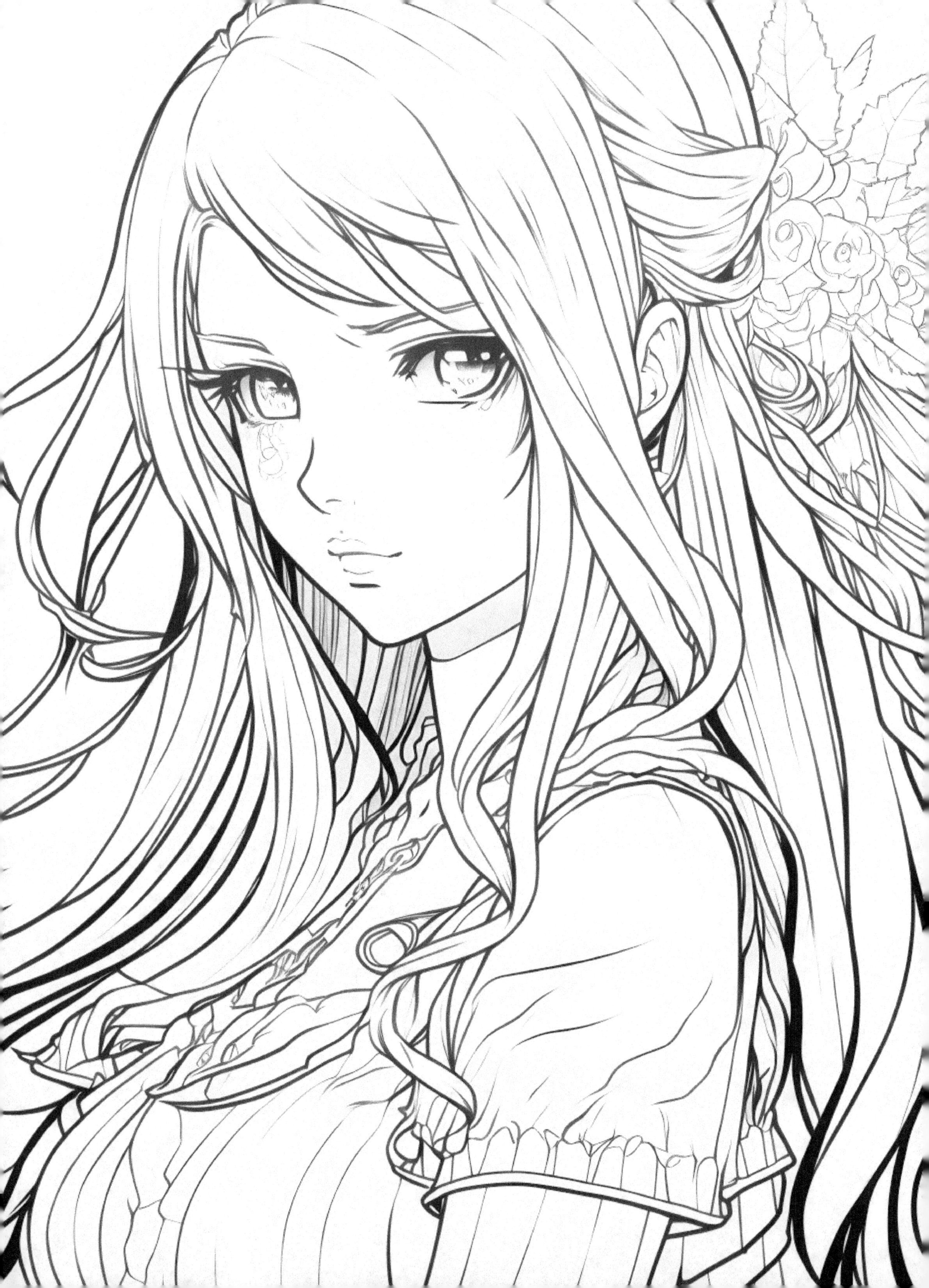

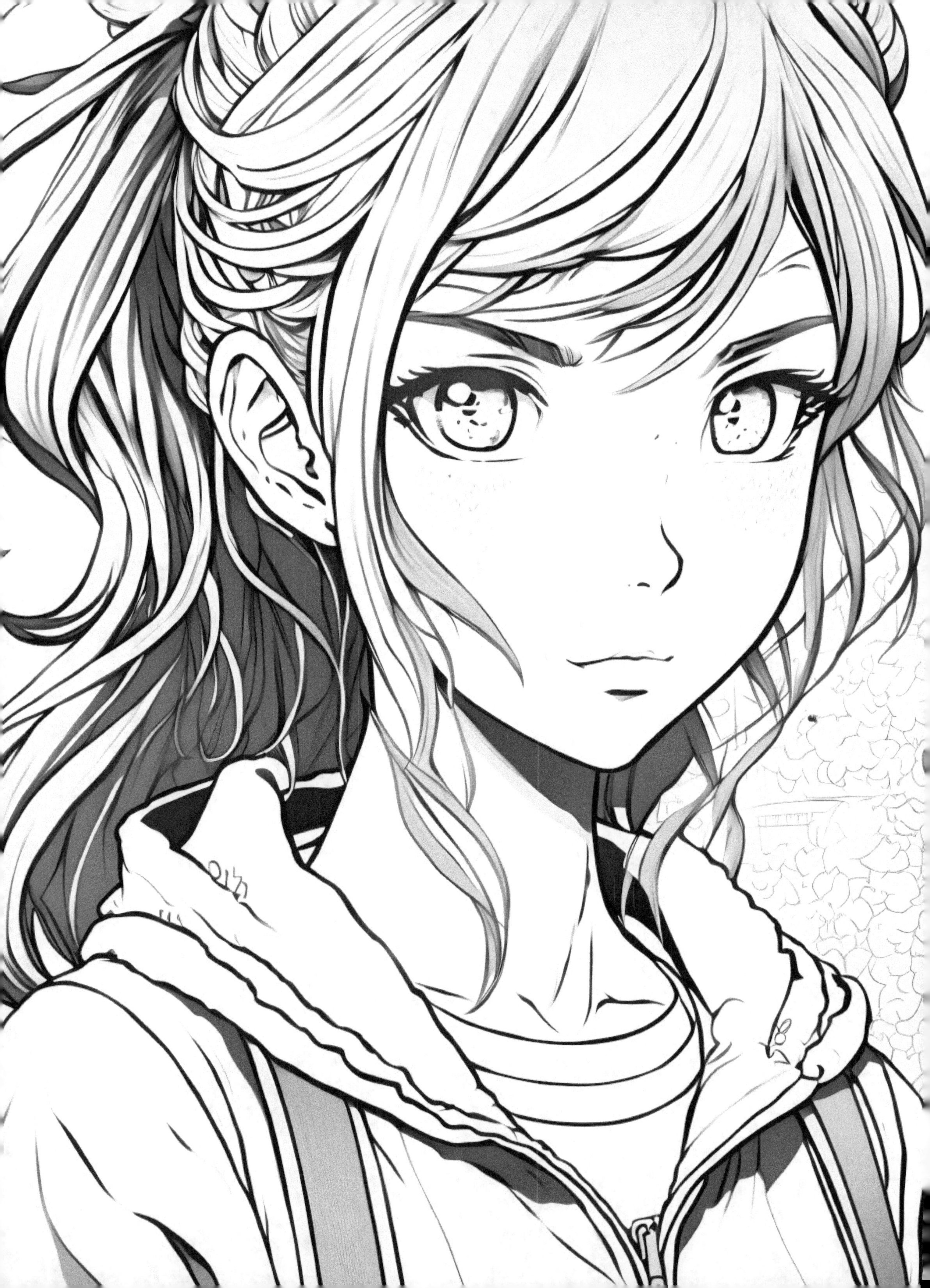

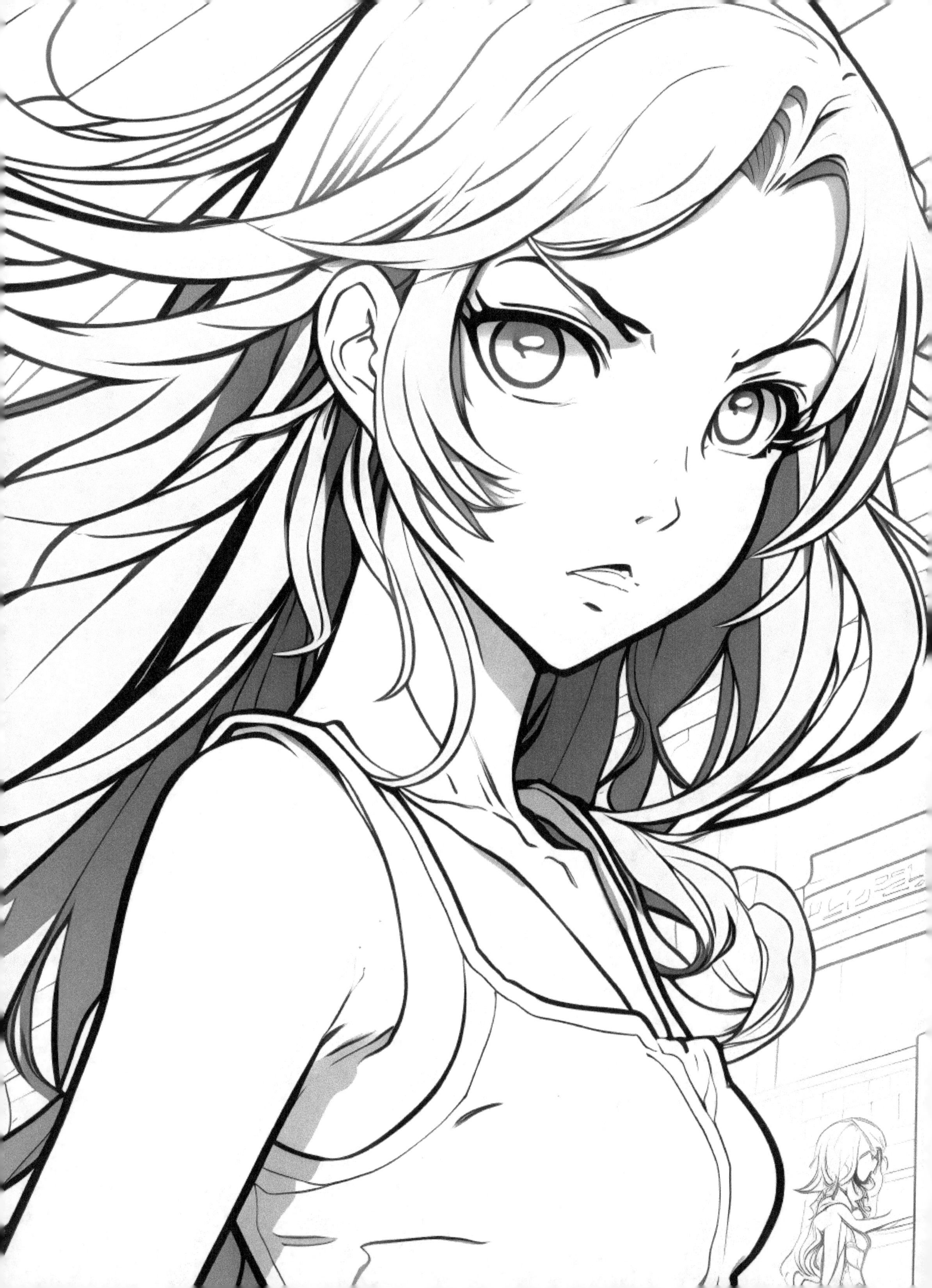

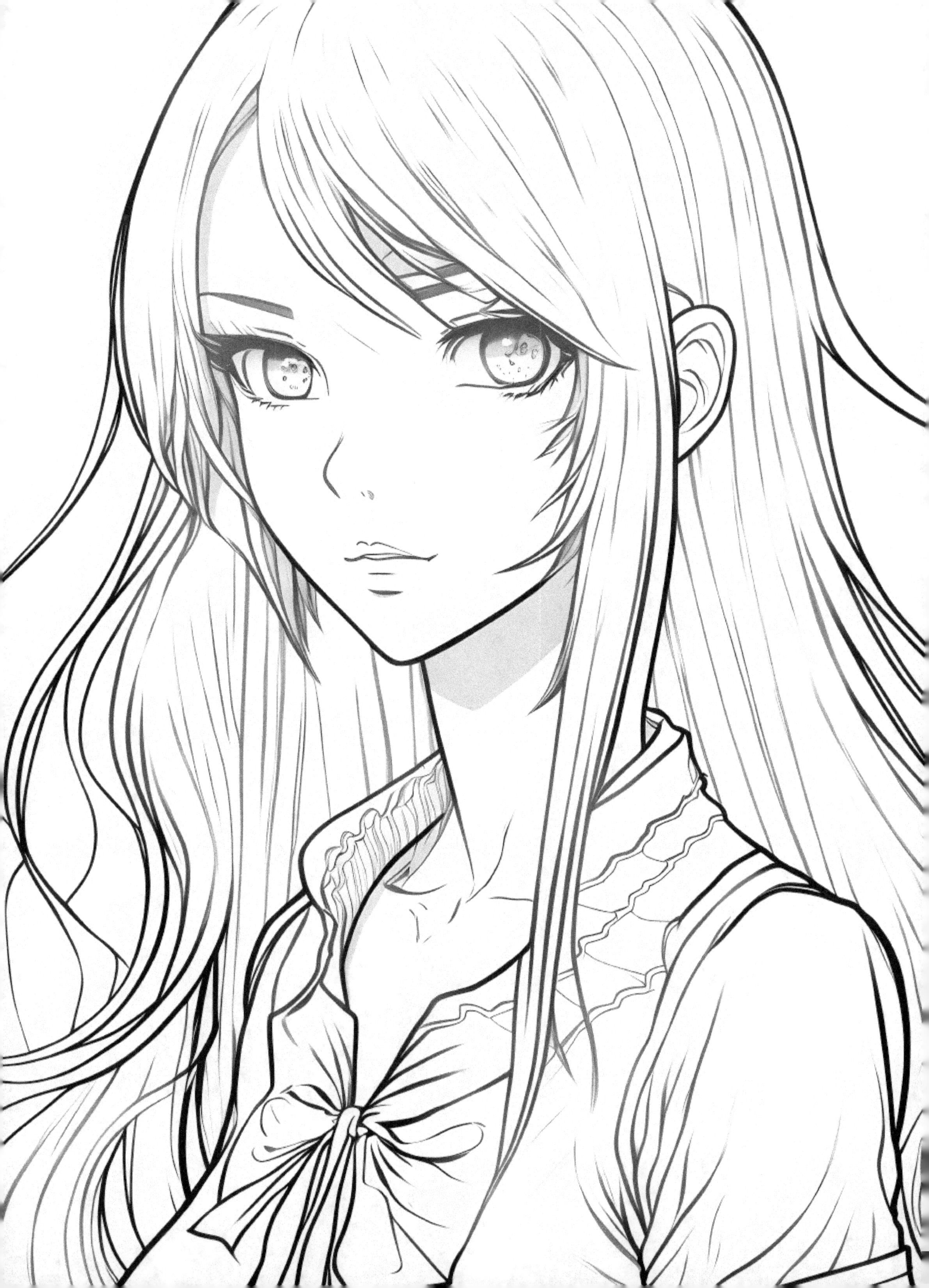

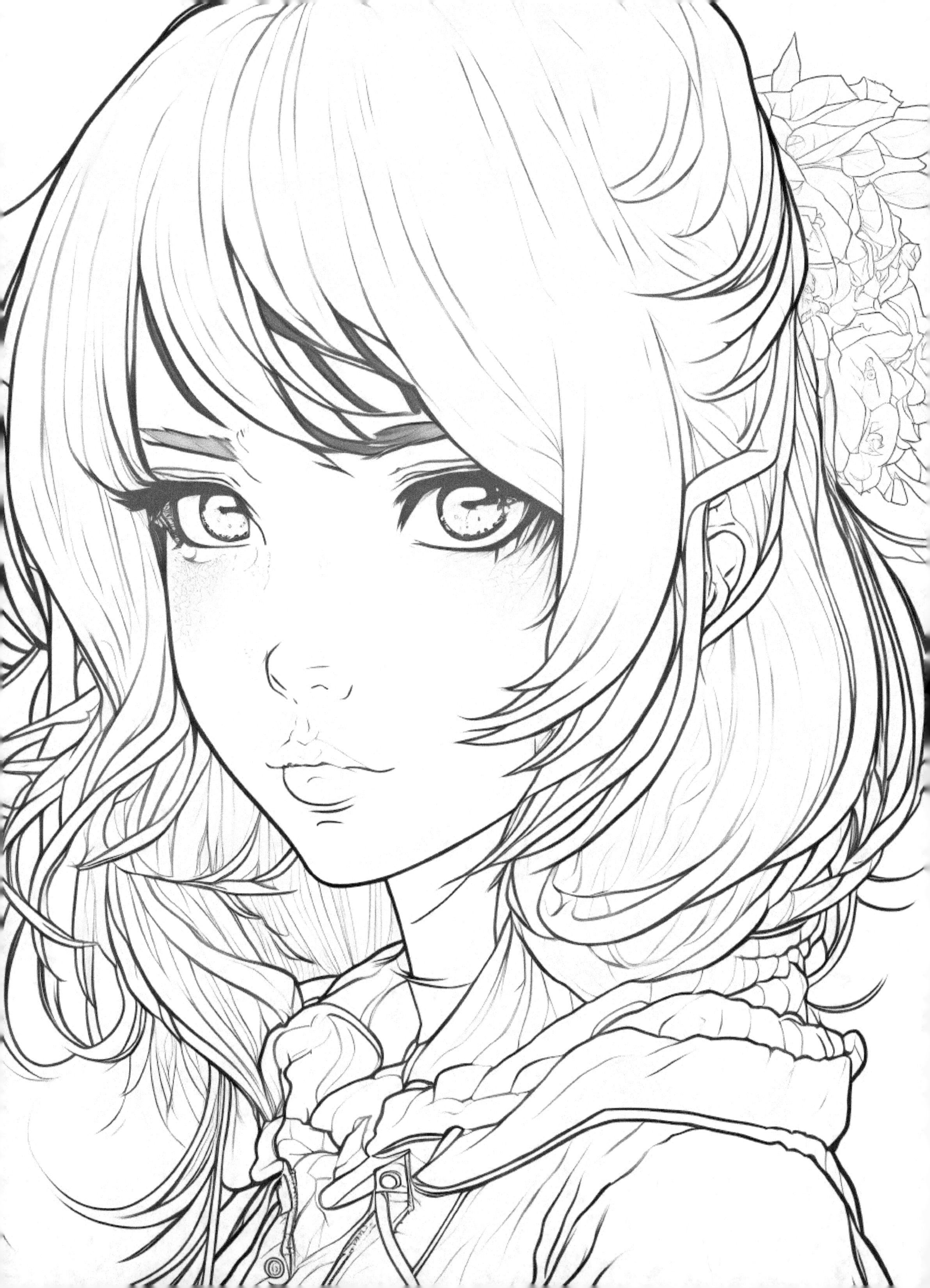

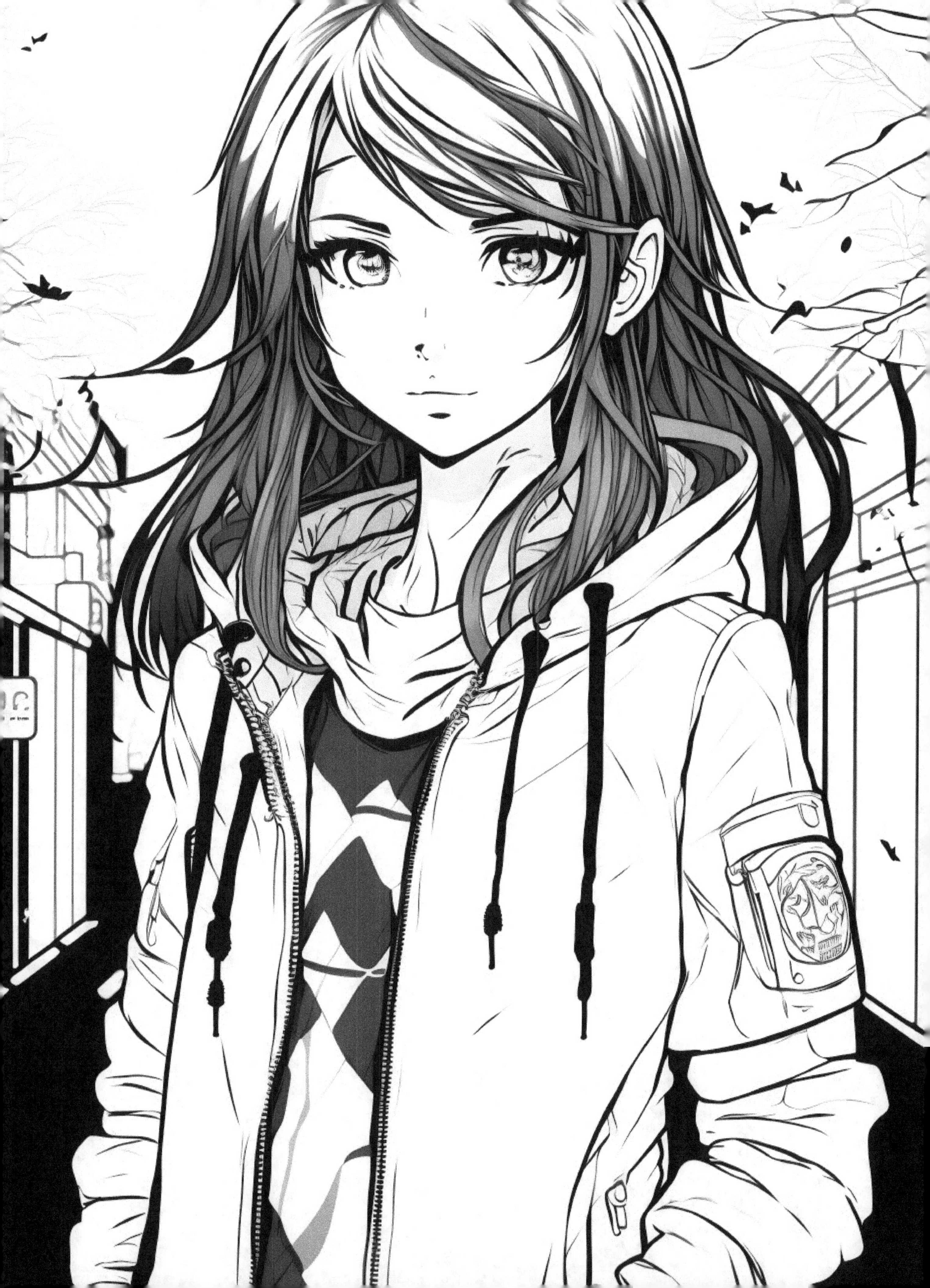

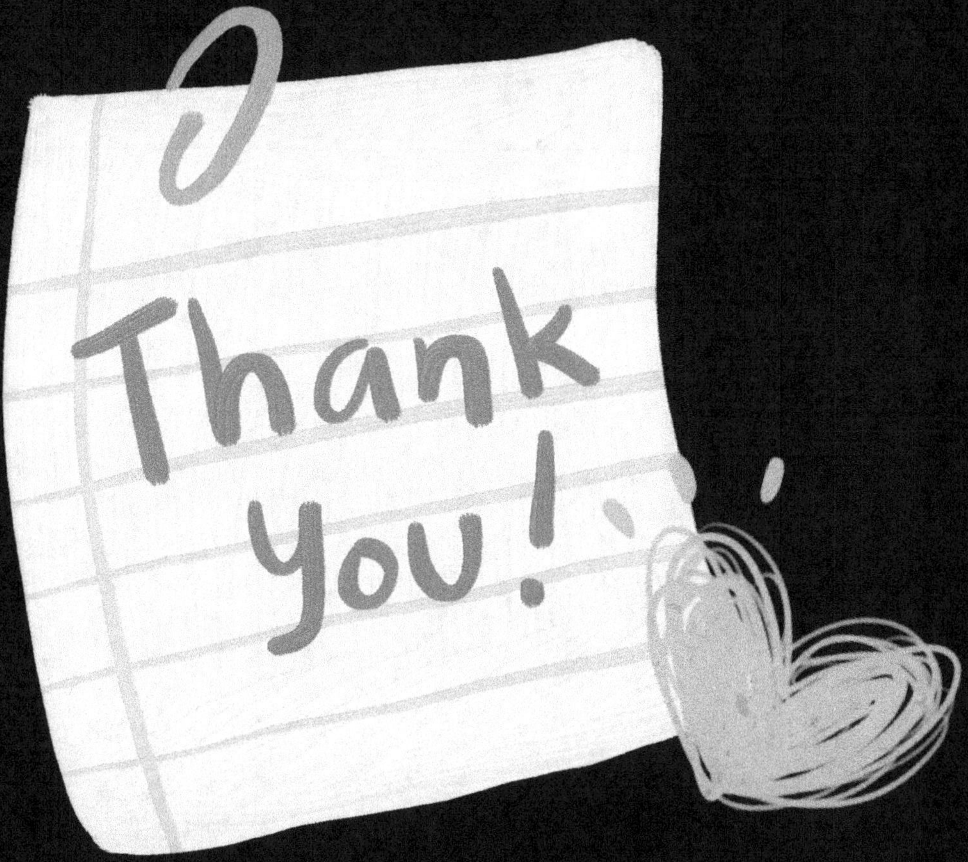

TOKYO STREETS

CAPI CAMP
ESTUDIOS

www.ingramcontent.com/pod-product-compliance
Lightning Source LLC
Chambersburg PA
CBHW080231220526
45467CB00037B/3145